Living Values Activities
for Children
Ages 8–14

Living Values Activities for Children Ages 8–14

DEVELOPED AND WRITTEN BY

Diane Tillman

WITH ADDITIONAL ACTIVITIES AND STORIES FROM
Pilar Quera Colomina
Lamia El-Dajani
Linda Heppenstall
Sabine Levy
Ruth Liddle
John McConnel
Marcia Maria Lins de Medeiros
and other educators around the world

Health Communications, Inc.
Deerfield Beach, Florida

www.hci-online.com

Visit the Living Values Web site for trainings at *http://www.livingvalues.net.*

Library of Congress Cataloging-in-Publication Data

Tillman, Diane
    Living values activities for children ages 8–14 / developed and written by Diane Tillman; with additional activities and stories from Pilar Quera Colomina . . . [et al.].
       p.   cm.
    Includes bibliographical references
    ISBN 1-55874-880-6 (trade paper : alk. paper)
    1. Moral education (Elementary) 2. Living Values, an Educational Program. 3. Values—Study and teaching (Elementary)—Activity programs. I. Quera Colomina, Pilar. II. Title.

LC268.T549 2000
370'.11'4—dc21

00-061412

Living Values: An Educational Program is a partnership among educators around the world. This program is supported by UNESCO and sponsored by the Spanish Committee of UNICEF, the Planet Society, and the Brahma Kumaris, in consultation with the Educational Cluster of UNICEF (New York).

Publisher: Health Communications, Inc.
             3201 S.W. 15th Street
             Deerfield Beach, FL 33442-8190

Cover and inside book design by Lawna Patterson Oldfield
Cover artwork by Frow Steeman
Inside artwork by Cicero Prado Sampaio
Original editors: Carol Gill, Irene Miller

CONTENTS

SETTING THE CONTEXT

INTRODUCTION

VALUES UNITS

APPENDIX

SETTING THE CONTEXT

The Call for Values

Children around the world are increasingly affected by violence, growing social problems and a lack of respect for each other and the world around them. Parents and educators in many countries are asking for help to turn around this alarming trend. Many of them believe part of the solution is an emphasis on teaching values. Living Values: An Educational Program (LVEP) has been produced in response to this call for values.

What Kind of Program Is LVEP?

Living Values: An Educational Program (LVEP) is a values education program. It offers a variety of experiential activities and practical methodologies for teachers and facilitators to help children and young adults explore and develop twelve key personal and social values: Cooperation, Freedom, Happiness, Honesty, Humility, Love, Peace, Respect, Responsibility, Simplicity, Tolerance and Unity. LVEP also contains special segments for use with parents and caregivers, as well as for refugees and children affected by war. As of March 2000, LVEP was already in use at over 1,800 sites in 64 countries. Reports from educators indicate that students are responsive to the values activities and become interested in discussing and applying values. Teachers note that students appear more confident, are more respectful to others, and exhibit an increase in positive and cooperative personal and social skills.

The Aims of LVEP:

- To help individuals think about and reflect on different values and the practical implications of expressing them in relation to themselves, others, the community and the world at large.
- To deepen understanding, motivation and responsibility with regard to making positive personal and social choices.
- To inspire individuals to choose their own personal, social, moral and spiritual values and be aware of practical methods for developing and deepening them.
- To encourage educators and caregivers to look at education as providing students with a philosophy of living, thereby facilitating their overall growth, development and choices so they may integrate themselves into the community with respect, confidence and purpose.

Current Status

LVEP is a nonprofit entity which is a partnership among educators around the world. It is currently supported by UNESCO and sponsored by the Spanish Committee of UNICEF, the Planet Society and the Brahma Kumaris, in consultation with the Education Cluster of UNICEF (New York).

This book contains activities for children ages eight to fourteen. Other components of Living Values: An Educational Program include five additional books: *Living Values Activities for Children Ages 3–7; Living Values Activities for Young Adults; LVEP Educator Training Guide; Living Values Parent Groups:*

Facilitator Guide; and *Living Values Activities for Refugees and Children Affected by War.*

Educators around the world are encouraged to utilize their own rich heritage while integrating values into everyday activities and the curriculum.

In the LVEP series, reflective and visualization activities encourage students to access their own creativity and inner gifts. Communication activities teach students to implement peaceful social skills. Artistic activities, songs and movement inspire students to express themselves while experiencing the value of focus. Gamelike activities are thought-provoking and fun; the discussion time that follows those activities helps students explore effects of different attitudes and behaviors. Other activities stimulate awareness of personal and social responsibility and social justice. The development of self-esteem and tolerance continues throughout the exercises.

LVEP materials have been translated into many languages. The current set of six books was developed from the Living Values Educators' Kit, originally available in English, French and Spanish. The expanded edition of the six LVEP books is currently available in English. Translation is ongoing in Arabic, Chinese, German, Greek, Hebrew, Hungarian, Italian, Japanese, Karen, Malay, Polish, Portuguese, Russian, Spanish, Thai, Turkish and Vietnamese.

Background

LVEP grew out of an international project begun in 1995 by the Brahma Kumaris to celebrate the fiftieth anniversary of the United Nations. Called Sharing Our Values for a Better World, this project focused on twelve universal values. The theme—adopted from a tenet in the Preamble of the United Nations' Charter—was: "To reaffirm faith in fundamental human rights, in the dignity and worth of the human person. . . ."

Living Values: A Guidebook was created as part of this project. It provided value statements on the twelve core values, offered an individual perspective for creating and sustaining positive change, and included facilitated group workshops and activities, including a small section of values activities for students in the classroom. That sketchy classroom curriculum became the inspiration and impetus for Living Values: An Education Initiative (LVEI).

LVEI was born when twenty educators from around the world gathered at UNICEF Headquarters in New York City in August 1996 to discuss the needs of children, their experiences of working with values and how educators can integrate values to better prepare students for lifelong learning. Using *Living Values: A Guidebook* and the "Convention on the Rights of the Child" as a framework, the global educators identified and agreed upon the purpose and aims of values-based education worldwide, in both developed and developing countries. The *Living Values Educators' Kit* was ready for piloting in February 1997, and Living Values has been gaining momentum ever since.

INTRODUCTION

Teaching Values

Living Values: An Educational Program values activities are designed to motivate students and to involve them in thinking about themselves, others, the world and values in ways that are relevant. They are designed to provoke the experience of values within and build inner resources. They are designed to empower and to elicit potential, creativity and inner gifts. Students are asked to reflect, imagine, dialogue, communicate, create, write about, artistically express and play with values. In the process, personal, social and emotional skills develop, as well as peaceful and cooperative social skills. The values have been arranged to provide a sequentially-based series of skills which build upon each other. The exercises include self-esteem building skills, positive social communication skills, critical thinking skills, and artistic and dramatic expression.

Three Core Assumptions

There are three core assumptions upon which LVEP is built:

1. Universal values teach respect and dignity for every person. Learning to enjoy those values promotes well-being for individuals and the larger society.

2. Each student does care about values and has the capacity to positively create and learn when provided with opportunities.

3. Students thrive in a values-based atmosphere in a positive, safe environment of mutual respect and care where students are regarded as capable of learning to make socially conscious choices.

These Living Values Activities can be utilized by school teachers, camp directors and parents. The adults involved are integral to the success of the program, for students learn by example and are most receptive when the information and learning points are congruent with the behaviors of the person sharing.

LVEP Trainings

The creation of a values-based atmosphere facilitates the success of this program, making it more enjoyable, beneficial and effective for both students and teachers. During LVEP trainings, educators participate in values awareness sessions. They are asked to reflect on their own values, offer their ideas on elements within a values-based atmosphere and imagine an optimal classroom environment. After teachers discuss their ideas on best teaching practices, LVEP's theoretical model and the rationale behind the variety of values activities are presented. This is followed by one or more sessions engaged in LVEP values activities for children and/or young adults. The workshop then turns to skills for creating a values-based environment: acknowledgement, encouragement, and positively building behaviors; active listening; conflict resolution; collaborative rule making; and values-based discipline.

Adults are asked to bring their own rich experiences into this initiative. The values activities contained in this section are only a beginning. Please expand on them with your own creativity and cultural and educational resources.

A Variety of Values Activities

It is not enough for students to hear about values. To really learn, they must experience them at many different levels, making them their own. And it is not enough to feel, experience and think about the values; social skills are needed to be able to use values throughout the day. The youngsters of today increasingly need to be able to see the effects of their behaviors and choices and be able to develop socially conscious decision-making skills. If the youth of today are going to carry these values not only into their personal lives as adults, but into the larger society, then it is also important to have them explore issues of social justice and have adult role models who exemplify those values.

Reflection Points

Reflection Points are at the beginning of every value unit and are incorporated in the lessons. They define values and offer some abstract concepts for reflection. There is a universal values perspective—that is, of valuing the dignity and worth of each human being and valuing the environment. For example, a point in the unit on Respect is: *Everyone in the world has the right to live with respect and dignity, including myself*. A Tolerance Reflection Point is: *Tolerance is being open and receptive to the beauty of differences*. Many of the Reflection Points are derived from *Living Values: A Guidebook*.

The teacher may wish to add a few of his or her own or use favorite sayings from the culture of the community and historical figures. Students can make up their own Reflection Points or research favorite sayings from their culture or history.

Imagining

A few values units ask students to imagine. For example, students are asked to imagine a peaceful world, to share their experiences and then to draw or paint a picture. This imagination exercise not only elicits the creativity of "good students," but also interests students often considered resistant or "unmotivated." Visualizing values in action makes them more relevant to students, as they find a place within where they can create that experience and think of ideas they know are their own.

Relaxation/Focusing Exercises

Very often students do not like "having to be quiet" in school. They seem to experience it as having to curtail their fun and repress their energy and enjoyment. It is viewed not as something enjoyable, but as something necessary to do in order to comply with adult requests. The Peace, Respect, Love and Freedom units introduce Relaxation/Focusing exercises. These are designed to help the students enjoy "feeling" the value. Teachers have found that doing these exercises help students quiet down, be more content and concentrate more successfully on their studies. Some teachers have found that students enjoy making up exercises of their own for the class.

Artistic Expression

Students are encouraged to reflect about values and experience them artistically and creatively through the arts. For example, they make slogans about peace and put them up on walls, or they sculpt freedom, draw simplicity or dance cooperation. As part of the activities about Simplicity, students are asked to take short walks in nature, write a poem to a tree and write a poem which the tree may write to them. While some songs are within the book, teachers are asked to bring in traditional songs of their culture or the cultures present in the area and to sing those with the students. Older students create poems and songs about values and bring in their current favorites.

Self-Development Activities

In these activities, students explore the value in relation to themselves or build skills in relation to the value. For example, students look at their own qualities during the unit on Respect as well as the types of words that give happiness to themselves and others. In one of the activities in the unit on Honesty, they examine their feelings when they are honest. There are a few stories about values, and teachers are encouraged to bring in their favorite stories on the unit of focus. Many of the values exercises require positive acknowledgment of students' responses.

Social Skills

Teachers are asked to teach and model conflict resolution skills. Suggestions are made for older students to become peace monitors on the playground. While there are many social skills included within these units, a few examples are: In the unit on Love, students explore ways to use words which others experience as flowers, not thorns. In the unit on Respect, older students examine subtle and not-so-subtle ways respect and disrespect are shown. Cooperation games are fun, yet elicit reflective comments. Students are asked to look at prejudice during the unit on Tolerance and to generate positive responses in social interactions.

Cognitive Awareness of Social Justice

Through exercises and questions, students are encouraged to look at the effect of an individual's actions on others and at how individuals can make a difference. For example, during the unit on Honesty, students are asked to make up a skit portraying the themes of honesty and dishonesty, taking the context from history or social studies. They then look for the effect of dishonesty or greed on others' lives and ask the actors how they felt. During history class, high school students are asked to look at the relationships among greed, corruption and the denial of human rights. During the unit on Simplicity, students are asked to examine the messages they get from the mass media and advertisements.

Developing Skills for Social Cohesion

The units on Tolerance, Simplicity and Unity bring in elements of social responsibility that are interesting and fun. Students explore the variety of cultures using the colors of a rainbow as an analogy. The unit on Simplicity includes suggestions for conservation and respect for the earth. Students explore positive examples of unity and then work together on a project of their choice.

Bringing in the Values of Your Culture

It is our hope that these activities will elicit ideas from teachers and parents as they explore with students the variety of ways to experience values. This material is intended to be a stimulus. Use your own resources and creativity. Adapt them to your group of students. Use materials that are easily available. Use your creativity, skills and knowledge to continue values-based education.

A variety of songs are included. However, since some of your students may not speak English, you may wish to translate the words or use songs from your own culture or different cultures from around the world.

A group of teachers may want to meet before the introduction of each value to share with each other their favorite stories for students about that value. Insert your stories at any time within the units. The students may enjoy enacting the stories. Ask the students to create their own plays and songs. They might even want to do a skit (sketch, play). Perhaps older adults can tell traditional tales and teach ancient forms of music.

Where Do I Begin?

While some teachers offer the values activities strictly in their own classrooms, many schools have found that a whole-school approach is very beneficial. In the latter instance, the staff will need to meet and may wish to include parents and a variety of people in different positions at the school site. Discuss your goals for the school, the needs of the students and the values on which you would like to focus. Some schools decide to focus on one value per month. Others choose several values for the entire year. This may depend on how frequently the values activities are done. Do them in order. For information on developing a school ethos, please refer to "A Blueprint: How to Introduce a Values-based Curriculum" in chapter 2 of the *LVEP Educator Training Guide.* Some schools have included parents as part of the program, using *Living Values Parent Groups: A Facilitator Guide.* Please refer to that guide for information on how to involve parents and caregivers in a values-based education program complementing the activities taught to the students.

Assemblies and Songs

If the entire school is exploring the same value for a period of time, a short assembly is often an excellent way to start. A few teachers could create the first program. After that, different classes of students could take turns doing a song and a skit. Or the principal may wish to tell a story and involve a few students from the audience.

Teachers and students are encouraged to select their own favorite songs on the value of focus. That would need to be done locally because of the diversity of languages, preferences of students at different ages and availability of materials.

Why Begin with the Peace and Respect Units?

It is important for each teacher, school, and/or school system to look at the needs of students and develop a program tailored to the particular setting. However, it is always suggested that you start with the Peace unit and follow that with the Respect unit. The Peace unit should be first, as our experience has been that all students are concerned about a peaceful world—even those students who may actively fight. Students appear to find the Peace unit relevant and interesting; it reduces "resistance" that teachers might otherwise encounter in students often considered "unmotivated." Respect is the second suggested values unit, as most students find it personally enhancing and helpful. Teachers find that the students become more confident, respectful to others and motivated in class.

Another reason we suggest these two units first is that the lessons they contain teach essential skills used throughout the other lessons. There are twenty-five lessons in the Peace unit and twenty-one lessons in the Respect unit. The Relaxation/Focusing exercises and conflict resolution skills developed during these lessons are important building blocks in creating both a values-based atmosphere and positive social skills.

A recommended order is noted below. However, students in different schools will have different needs. Hence, while Peace and Respect should always be first, choose which values units you would like to do next. A few of the values units pair up well, complementing each other. Below you will note recommendations regarding the order of those pairs and a couple of remarks about timing.

Recommended Order of Values Units

1. Peace — This unit has the most lessons and needs the most time.

2. Respect

3. Love — Love further develops skills from Peace and Respect.

4. Tolerance — Love should come before Tolerance. So third and fourth is a good order; however, Tolerance can be done later.

5. Happiness

6. Responsibility — It is a good idea to do Happiness before Responsibility.

7. Cooperation — Cooperation can be the third value or done any time thereafter.

8. Humility — Humility and Honesty are a good pair. Short units, they can be done concurrently.

9. Honesty

10. Simplicity — Good with your study of native cultures and the environment.

11. Freedom — Do Responsibility before Freedom.

12. Unity — Perfect to do as the last values unit.

When Do I Have Time to Teach Values?

Some schools create a special "Values Time." The educators who have done that looked closely at their program to find how the values activities could fit into an existing time slot. For example, one school found that it fit into the first short period of "home room." Another found there was a twenty-minute "integration time" for building relationships between students with different languages. Some teachers use the lessons while teaching English as a Second Language. For many schools, however, the schedule is already over-full and the regular curriculum looks like more than enough.

Given the many benefits of teaching values, many educators are finding ways to incorporate values activities within their day. History, social studies and literature lead themselves easily to an exploration of values, as do the arts. As many of the activities in this book fit into the liberal arts curriculum, some schools create most of their "values time" during the language arts time slot. Other values activities fit into social studies units, art, drama or physical education.

At schools where one teacher is with a group of students for an entire day, the teacher can readily assess into which subject area a particular lesson fits. At schools where students attend several different classes with different instructors, a team of teachers may wish to brainstorm values applications at their particular site. Perhaps the language arts and expressive arts teachers will take up the values units of Peace, Respect and Responsibility for several months, while social studies teachers will take up the major values focus on Honesty.

Acknowledging Responses

Occasionally there are students who are resistant to school and/or schoolwork, and that may include values activities initially. Part of resistance may be anger at not being heard and at not feeling adequate or valued. Part of the success of these values activities is acceptance of each student.

Acceptance and acknowledgment of students' responses are essential components of many discussions that take place as part of the values activities. This may pose a challenge to teachers who are accustomed to having only "right" or "wrong" answers in the classroom. While there are "right" and "wrong" answers in math and science, for instance, a student's emotional feeling about a concept is simply his or her own.

Resistant students may initially test the acceptance of their answers by giving nonstandard responses. For example, when asked about a peaceful world, a student might say, "War has to be part of a peaceful world." Or, in response to a question in the Happiness unit about what he or she likes to hear, a student might respond, "I like to hear that I am bad." Simply consider these responses as reflections of the student's unhappiness. Nod with respect, just as you did to the other students.

It is sufficient to nod, but a verbal response acknowledging the student's answer and restating the content of his or her message is a more effective method of giving respect. Consistently receiving respect from an adult in this way frees the student from the trap of blaming the adult for not understanding. Actively listening to such responses allows the student to accept her or his emotions and begin to process them. For example, if the student draws guns in her picture of a peaceful world, the teacher might say in an accepting manner, if the child's face seems tense, "It must be a little scary if there are guns even in a peaceful world." (Please refer to the section on "Active Listening" in the *LVEP Educator Training Guide* for more on this topic.)

It is important for the educator to be consistent in modeling his or her own values. At some point in the lesson, you may wish to add your own positive answer and why you believe that. Students are generally curious about teachers and are interested in a teacher's passion for something noble/

good/true. When this is done, resistance does fade, and the student's natural qualities begin to emerge.

When Students Insist They Are Bad

Sometimes older students may insist they like something or someone that does harm, for example, choosing to admire a negative figure. If this comes up during a discussion (though it might be better to address on a one-on-one basis) ask, "Why do you admire that person?" "What do you think that person would like to see happen?" "Why?" "What is the value under that?" Continue to query, focusing closer and closer on the original intention. There is always a positive value or quality under the original intention.

When this is done, the teacher can affirm, "So, you admire _____," making note of the positive value. This is said with the understanding that people do wrong things, but somewhere there is a good motive. It may not be well-thought-out, it may have disastrous consequences for other people, but somewhere there was a good intention. The purpose of taking this approach with a student is to align him or her with a positive value or positive purpose. They can change their own view of themselves as "bad" if there is acceptance of a positive value or caring about something. Nurture that kernel in positive ways, and the student can begin to view himself or herself differently.

Students are encouraged to think, to look at consequences, and to develop emotional awareness and problem-solving skills in this program. Allow them space to explore and make their own decisions. Then they will make wiser decisions—and not only when adults are watching!

Incorporating Values into the Existing Curriculum

Many schools focus on one value for a particular length of time, often one or two months. All teachers are encouraged to incorporate some values exploration into the regular curriculum. History, social studies and literature lend themselves easily to the teaching of values. During history and social studies lessons, ask students to recognize and discuss the application of a particular value or the consequences due to lack of that value. For example, a historical unit about independence is an ideal time to examine what type of freedom these people wanted. During literature, books and stories could be selected in which the heroine or hero demonstrates the value being studied. Students could write about values, create poems and dramas about values and express values in their art projects.

Values webs—appropriate to the culture—are useful. Start with the stimulus, ask the students to discuss the value in the context of the subject and then incorporate that in the follow-up activity. An example of a values web on Freedom follows.[1]

Using Values Activities for Second Language Acquisition

Several teachers around the world reported using values activities while teaching English as a Second Language. They found that students enjoyed the activities; their interest in class discussions and activities increased. While many of the values activities contain discussion questions, the teacher may wish make a few adaptations if the activities are to be used in language acquisition classes. Such might include expanding and making some of the questions more concrete, playing songs more than once, asking students to identify tenses, and providing practice in receptive and expressive language skills, etc.

Values Web

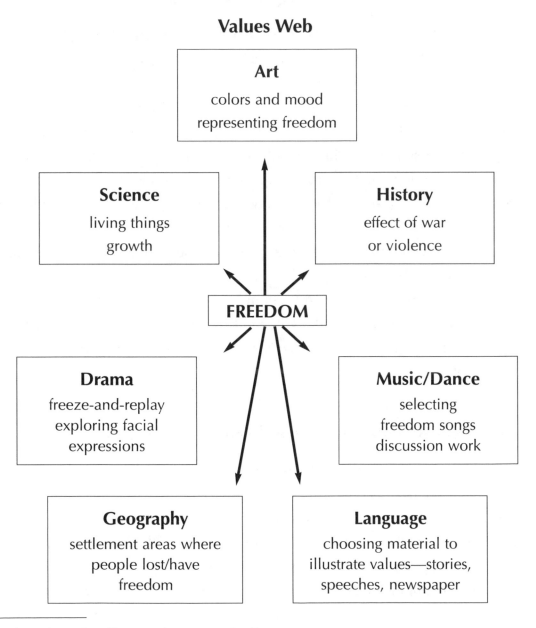

As an example of this, an educator from New Zealand, Trish Summerfield, submitted the following lesson plan. Using a song in the Peace unit, she encourages students to contemplate values and use them to create a more positive classroom and world environment. Together with this, the material is used in a way that develops the students' overall acquisition of a second language.

Level: Elementary/pre-intermediate language skill level, or special needs secondary students.

Goal: To explore values while developing second language skills.

Values-Based Objective: For students to consider values required to make their classroom and world a better place.

Learning-Based Objectives:

- Development of listening skills using a listening cloze.
- Development of the skill of taking dictation while a song is playing.
- Development of oral skills through singing and discussing the song and its values.
- Development of reading skills through reading a song and answering questions based on the song.
- Development of new vocabulary from the song.

Grammar Used: Past simple, present simple, present continuous and present perfect.

Resources: A recording of "Imagine" by John Lennon and a written copy of the lyrics.

Reflection: Write "John Lennon" on the board. Ask the students:

- Who is he?
- Is he alive?

- What songs did he sing?
- What music group did he belong to?
- What were his songs about?

Teach new vocabulary words in the song.

Visualization

Give the students a cloze listening sheet on the song. Play it two times. Review the answers on the board. Alternatively, a jigsaw cloze may be used for the students to review the song in pairs.

Play the song again for the students to sing as a group.

Ask the students to turn the cloze sheet over and work in pairs to do a running dictation of the song. Place copies of the song at the front of the room. This exercise may also be done in groups of three, which is more difficult but more fun. Students then review their dictation using the completed cloze sheet.

Understanding

Comprehension Exercises—Written:

- Would there be hunger in John Lennon's vision of a perfect world?
- Would there be war in John Lennon's vision of a perfect world?
- What would there be in this world?
- What wouldn't there be in this world?

Comprehension Exercises—Pair work oral discussion:

- Have you ever heard this song before? When?
- Do you like this song? Why/Why not?
- Is this song popular in your country of origin?
- How did you feel when you listened to the song?

- Would you like to live in such a world? Why/Why not?
- How can we make our world like the world in the song?

Make a list of things we can do to make our world better. (Younger students may enjoy making these lists into a poster that could be displayed in the classroom.)

Teacher Note: If oral skill development is the focus, students could change partners and share their lists with new partners, taking note of the ideas that are the same.

Expression

Students could do these exercises in pairs or individually, in the classroom or as a homework assignment.

What values were in the song? What was your favorite value in the song? How can people practice that value?

Write sentences using the new vocabulary.

Make a list of all the verbs in the song. Make a list of all the adjectives in the song.

Assessment

Listening close.

Informal monitoring of the oral discussion.

Marking the extension writing for grammar and vocabulary.

Unifying/Summarizing Board

At a site where students have most of their values activities in one classroom, a unifying and summarizing activity would be to make a large, leafless tree on a bulletin board with an oval seed below the trunk. The seed should be large enough to contain the names of the values on which the class is working. As the students work with each value, write that value on a different color paper and put it in the seed. As students finish their unit on each value, individuals or small groups could write on leaves of the matching color their conclusions about the effects of that value. Freedom could be green, with the students recording the fruits of freedom on green leaves. Respect might be blue. As the units continue, the tree—with its rainbow of colored leaves—would develop, summarizing the students' thoughts and providing a group memory and reference point.

Symbols Used Throughout the Lessons

 Discuss/share

 Sing or play a song

 Relaxation/focusing exercise

 Read a story selection from a book

 Imagining Exercise

 Artistic expression

 Creative or reflective writing

 Skill building or cooperative activity

Note to Teacher

♦ Denotes a Reflection Point

Sometimes a couple of follow-up options are offered as part of the values lessons. "Eight to Ten Activity" means it is suggested for eight- to ten-year-olds. Age suggestions are approximate. Feel free to choose the level of follow-up activity that you feel is most appropriate for your group of students.

Students and Educators—Share with the World!

Students

Students usually enjoy sharing their creations. Students around the world are invited to share their thoughts, poems, essays, songs, drawings, activities and experiences with students of similar age through the Living Values web site. Visit *www.livingvalues.net* and click on "Children Participate."

Educators Share

Adults using LVEP are also invited to share their experiences. You may share your activities and expertise with other educators around the world through the Living Values web site. Or send in your contribution to the nearest LVEP Country Coordinator.

Annual Evaluation

An important part of any program is evaluation. Your evaluation of the program and observations about changes with students are very important. Kindly let the LVEP Coordinator in your country know you are using LVEP, and you will be sent an Educator Evaluation Form annually. Or you may fill out this form on the web site.

We hope you enjoy Living Values. Thank you.

ONE

1. PEACE UNIT

3

Peace

Peace Reflection Points

♦ Peace is more than the absence of war.

♦ Peace is living in harmony and not fighting with others.

♦ If everyone in the world were peaceful, this would be a peaceful world.

♦ Peace is being quiet inside.

♦ Peace is a calm and relaxed state of mind.

Peace

Peace consists of positive thoughts, pure feelings and good wishes.

Peace begins within each one of us.

To stay peaceful requires strength and compassion.

Peace is a qualitative energy that brings balance.

World Peace grows through nonviolence, acceptance, fairness and communication.

Peace is the main characteristic of a civilized society.

"Peace must begin with each one of us. Through quiet and serious reflection on its meaning, new and creative ways can be found to foster understanding, friendships and cooperation among all peoples." —Javier Perez de Cuellar, Former Secretary-General of the United Nations.

Peace Unit

GOAL: To experience peace for the self.
OBJECTIVES:

❑ To think about and appreciate peace.

❑ To experience what peace feels like and to draw or write about it.

❑ To identify what allows the students to feel peaceful.

❑ To write a poem or short story about their most peaceful moments.

❑ To enjoy being quiet and peaceful during Relaxation/Focusing exercises in the classroom.

❑ To help students increase their ability to concentrate.

❑ To express peace artistically.

❑ To sing two songs about peace.

GOAL: To increase knowledge about the components of a peaceful world.

OBJECTIVES:

- ❏ To imagine a peaceful world and communicate their ideas through words and a drawing or a short essay.
- ❏ To identify differences between a peaceful world and a world of conflict.
- ❏ To select ten items which represent a peaceful world.
- ❏ To participate in making a World Cake of human qualities, choosing the qualities that they think are most important for a Peaceful World and sharing the results with their family.
- ❏ To participate in making a "Feelings of Peace" collage.

GOAL: To build positive, peaceful methods of dealing with conflict, including conflict resolution skills.

OBJECTIVES:

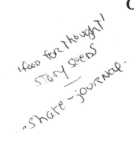

- ❏ To participate in a discussion about how they feel when people are mean or hurtful.
- ❏ To think of consequences of peace and war.
- ❏ To be able to listen to others during a conflict resolution exercise and repeat key phrases of what they say.
- ❏ To participate in a conflict resolution exercise, stating how they feel and identifying what they would like others to do and not do. They may participate by playing a role in the exercise, as a participant in a real conflict or as a peer mediator.
- ❏ To demonstrate understanding of how hurt or fear moves into anger by being able to state two examples.

eace

❏ To identify two thoughts or actions that allow negativity to grow.

❏ To identify two thoughts or actions that allow peace to grow.

❏ To create a story or study about peace heroes.

Peace Lessons

Peace is often the first value introduced in a school or classroom. If the entire school is doing a values program, your school may wish to have an assembly on peace.

Play a song about peace every day at the beginning of "values time." Choose a song you feel the students will relate to and one that is appropriate for their age. One peace song is "Teaching Peace" by Red and Kathy Grammer. Favorites with older students are "Imagine" by John Lennon and "We Are the World" by USA for Africa. You may want the students to bring in songs that relate to the theme.

PEACE LESSON 1

Imagining a Peaceful World

Play a song on peace. Explain that in the next few weeks the school/class will be exploring something very important, peace.

Discuss/Share

- Who can tell me about peace?
- What is peace?
- What does it mean to have a peaceful world?

Peace

Acknowledge all responses and thank them for sharing. Continue with Imagining a Peaceful World exercise.

Imagining a Peaceful World

Lead the students in this imagining exercise. Say the following, pausing at the dots:

"A wonderful thing about people your age is that each one knows about peace. I'd like to start our unit by asking you to use your mind to imagine a peaceful world. Let yourself be very still. I want you to picture in your mind a beautiful, big bubble. This bubble is so big that you can step inside. It's like a small, silent plane that you can travel in to imagine going into the future, to a better world. . . . You step inside the bubble and float to that world that is completely peaceful. . . . The bubble rests on the ground of this world, and you step out. . . . What does it look like there? . . . Imagine how you would feel. . . . How does nature look? . . . What is the air like? . . . How do the houses look? . . . As you take a walk around a lake, let yourself feel how peaceful that place is and how you feel. . . . Look in the lake and see your reflection. . . . You can feel your body relaxing in this peaceful place. . . . As you pass by a group of people, notice the expressions on their faces and how they relate to one another. . . . A group of people smile and wave as you step back into your bubble plane to return here. . . . The bubble floats back to this time and this class. . . . As you experience yourself seated here, the bubble disappears, leaving you with a feeling of stillness within."

Discuss/Share

Give the students time to share their visualization. Some may wish to share their experience. Or the teacher may wish to ask them to share first about nature, then themselves, and then about what they imagined about relationships with others.

PEACE LESSON 2

A Peaceful World

Lesson
2

Begin with a song on peace. You may want to teach a song to the younger students. Play a song for the older students to which they will relate. Ask them to bring in a couple of their favorite recordings.

Explain that you would like them to imagine a peaceful world again, and then write or draw their experience.

Do the Imagining a Peaceful World exercise again.

Eight to Eleven Activity: Divide the class into small groups of students, so each group can draw a large picture of a peaceful world. If this is done just after the above visualization, it is sometimes interesting for them to do it silently. Ask the students afterward, "What kind of words and behavior helped everyone stay peaceful?" Ask each group of students to bring its large picture up to the front and talk about it to the rest of the class.

Twelve to Fourteen Activity: Ask them to share their thoughts about a peaceful world in writing. Or they may write a few lines and illustrate them.

Peace

PEACE LESSON 3

A World of Peace Versus a World of Conflict

Explain: "Today I would like you to think about the differences between a peaceful world and a world of conflict. What kinds of things exist in a world of conflict that do not exist in a world of peace?" Students are likely to name war, guns, gangs.

Activity

Make two columns on the board and label them Actions in a Peaceful World and Actions in a World of Conflict. Generate ideas for each list.

Ten to Fourteen Activity: Instruct the students to make a Mind Map of a Peaceful World. They could make a Mind Map of a World of Conflict the next day. To begin a Mind Map, each student makes a small image or picture in the middle of a blank piece of paper. They then draw several lines outward, adding smaller lines to those. On each line, students are to put different aspects of their image/concept in the center of the page. Ask them to make one sheet for a Peaceful World and another Mind Map for a World of Conflict.

If the students have not done Mind Mapping before, the teacher will need to introduce it, using the information on Mind Mapping in the Appendix (Item 2).

Play or sing a peace song.

Peace

Discuss the Reflection Points:

♦ Peace is more than the absence of war.
♦ Peace is living in harmony and not fighting with others.
♦ If everyone in the world were peaceful, this would be a peaceful world.

PEACE LESSON 4

Time Capsule

Say, "Today let's pretend that you are living in the peaceful world that you imagined the other day, and you are asked to make a time capsule to let future generations know your world. What ten items would you choose to put in that time capsule to let them know more about a peaceful world?" The students could work individually, in pairs or in small groups.

PEACE LESSON 5

If We Were All Peaceful

Song

Play, teach or sing with the students a peace song from your particular culture, or share your favorite peace song.

Write the Reflection Points on the board:

♦ Peace is being quiet inside.
♦ Peace is a calm and relaxed state of mind.

♦ Peace consists of positive thoughts, pure feelings and good wishes.

Discuss/Share

- If every single person in this world were peaceful inside, would this world be more peaceful? How?
- What does peace feel like?

Introduce the Physical Relaxation exercise: Say, "Many people in the world today feel very stressed. Have you ever heard any adults say they are stressed? Well, one of the ways to help get rid of stress and feel more peaceful is doing a Physical Relaxation exercise. When we get rid of some tension, we can be at our best. Let's try it." Play some relaxing music, if possible.

Physical Relaxation Exercise

"Sit comfortably . . . and relax. . . . As you relax, let your body feel heavy and focus your attention on your feet. . . . Tighten all your muscles for a moment . . . and then relax them. . . . Let them stay relaxed. . . . Now become aware of your legs, letting them be heavy . . . tightening the muscles . . . and then relaxing them. . . . Now your stomach. . . . Tighten the muscles for a moment . . . and then relax them. . . . Free any tension. . . . Be aware of your breathing, and let yourself breathe slowly and deeply. . . . Breathe deeply, letting the air out slowly. . . . Now tighten the muscles in your back and your shoulders . . . and then relax them. . . . Let your hands and arms tighten . . . and then relax them. . . . Gently move your neck . . . first to one side, then the other. . . . Relax the muscles. . . . Now tighten the muscles of your face . . . your jaw . . . and then relax your face and your jaw. . . . Let the feeling of well-being flow through your body. . . . Focus again on breathing, taking in clear air, letting out any remaining tension. . . . I am relaxed . . . in a state of well-being . . . and ready to be at my best."

—Contributed by Guillermo Simó Kadletz

Eight to Ten Activity: Choose one color and draw peace.
Eleven to Fourteen Activity: Write about a time you felt really peaceful.

PEACE LESSON 6

Baking a World Cake

Lesson
6

Make a World Cake of human qualities and characteristics. This activity provides an opportunity for students to think about a better world, create and discuss what they think is important with their peers, parents and teachers. (Students can work in pairs or in small groups to bake the cake.)

Discuss/Share

- What are the finest human qualities you think should be in the World Cake?
- Would all the ingredients be pure, or would you include some "not so good" ingredients to remind us we need to work together to remove those items that cause harm or hurt?

Peace

Activity

Step 1. Choose the ingredients. Make a list of the finest human qualities you would like to put into your World Cake.

Step 2. Choose the amount of each ingredient. The amount of each ingredient can be measured in grams, kilograms, tons, percentages or any other suitable way.

Step 3. Mixing and baking the cake. Describe the order in which you would put the ingredients into the cake mix and explain how you would mix and bake the cake. (The evening before Lesson 6, younger students may wish to look at a recipe book with their father or mother.)

For an example of a World Cake created by a student in China, see Item 1 in the Appendix.

End Lesson 6 with a peace song.

Lesson 7

PEACE LESSON 7

Baking a World Cake Continues

Activity

Step 3 continued. Continue creating the ingredients and writing down their order.

Step 4. Presenting your work. You can record your work in any way you wish. Your presentation can be as simple, imaginative, creative and illustrated as you wish. (If the students have worked individually, an extra day may be needed.)

Step 5. Sharing your work. Talk about your World Cake with family and friends. Explain that the ingredients and the way it is

Peace

baked make it taste the way it does. Invite them to share their feelings about your cake.

Display. Put your work in a folder, on the wall or in shop windows in the community.

Another possibility: Send copies of your recipes to the World Peace Messenger Organization at the United Nations.

—Contributed by Peter Williams

PEACE LESSON 8

A Special Place

Lesson
8

Discuss/Share

- Do you have a special place where you can sit quietly and think?
- Why do we need to be quiet and peaceful sometimes?
- How do you feel inside when you are quiet and peaceful?
- What sorts of things prevent us from feeling peaceful?

—West Kidlington School

Discuss the Reflection Point: Peace consists of positive thoughts, pure feelings and good wishes.

Peaceful Star Relaxation Exercise

Read the following slowly, pausing at the ellipses.

"One way to be peaceful is to be silent inside. For a few moments, think of the stars and imagine yourselves to be just like them. They are so beautiful in the sky, and they sparkle and shine. They are so quiet and peaceful. Let your body be still. . . . Relax your toes and legs. . . . Relax your stomach . . . and your shoulders. . . . Relax your arms . . . and your face. . . . Let the feeling of being safe emerge . . . and a soft light of peace surround you. . . . Inside you are like a beautiful little star. . . . You, the tiny star inside, are full of peaceful light . . . This light is soft and safe. . . . Relax into that light of peace and love. . . . Let yourself be still and peaceful inside. . . . You are focused . . . concentrated. . . . Whenever you want to feel peaceful inside, you can become still . . . content . . . a star of peace."

Activity

Ask students to write a short story or a poem about their most peaceful moments. "I feel most peaceful when . . ."

PEACE LESSON 9

Increasing Peace at School

Begin with a song.

Introduction: "The other day we made a list of the differences between a peaceful world and a world of conflict. Today, I'd like you to think about the differences between a peaceful school and a school with conflict." Ask:

- What kinds of things would happen in each of those schools?
- How do the people feel who are fighting?
- How do the people feel in the peaceful school?

Say, "Just as people create their world and students create

what happens on the playground, so we are creating what happens here in this class." Ask:

- What kind of classroom do you want?
- Is there anything you would like to try to make our class more peaceful?

Listen respectfully to all their suggestions. Ask them to select one they would like to try. For younger students, help them make the suggestions practical, e.g., after lunch, we could play a peace song, or we could really listen when other people are sharing. Try the idea and ask the students to evaluate the process. Allow them to decide if they want to try it for another day.

PEACE LESSON 10

Feelings of Peace Collage

Lesson

10

Begin with the Peaceful Star exercise.

NOTE TO TEACHER
All relaxation/focusing exercises can be found in the Appendix.

Discuss/Share

What symbols represent peace to you?

Activity

As the students think about what peace means to them, instruct them to make an image or an object or to search through magazines they have collected for photos, pictures or symbols that illustrate a world of peace. Tell them this is the start of building a collage. Ask them to begin a collage with images, drawings and photos. Suggest they continue to add new symbols, details and words that illustrate this world of peace.

—Contributed by Sabine Levy

PEACE LESSON 11

Words of Peace

Discuss the Reflection Points:

- ◆ Peace is a qualitative energy that brings balance.
- ◆ World Peace grows through nonviolence, acceptance, fairness and communication.
- ◆ Peace is the main characteristic of a civilized society.

Activity

Continue work on the collage. Some students may have brought things from home to add.

Allow students to generate their own commentaries about how they see peace, contributing images that express peace. Post their commentaries or short poems on the collage.

Do one of the relaxation exercises.

—Contributed by Pilar Quera Colomina

Peace

PEACE LESSON 12

Arms Are For . . .

Tell the students that today you would like them to think about arms.

- What are arms? What are they used for?

They will probably tell you about their two bodily arms. So talk about what those arms can do. "They can hug, pick up things, cook, paint beautiful paintings, throw footballs, work to make homes and tall buildings, help sick animals, etc. Linking arms is a sign of closeness and being friends. Arms can also push, shove and fight. How we use our arms is what creates peace or conflict. How we use our arms makes a difference." Ask:

- How do you feel when others use their arms to hurt you or someone you care about? (Acknowledge and accept all answers and reflect their feelings. Comment, "Yes, it is painful when others hurt us.")

If one of the students has not already mentioned it, tell them the word arms is synonymous with the word weapons. Human arms have been used to make guns and weapons of war. Arms to destroy things are simply an extension of the person who has the bodily arms and decides to create something that can destroy. Ask:

- Why do you think people start wars?
- What would you like to tell them?

P

Acknowledge all their ideas.

Say, "There's a slogan: Arms are for hugging, not for shoving." Ask:

- Can you think of other slogans about arms? (Give an example or two if they do not generate some. Examples are: Arms are for giving, not for grabbing. Arms are for use, not for abuse. Arms are for holding, not for hurting. Have fun making some up.)
- Can you think of a slogan you could say to someone if someone was bothering you?

 Comment: "People need to know that it is not right to hurt others." Write down what they come up with and save it on the board for use in another lesson. Ask:

- Can anyone think of another slogan for peace?

Activity

Ask them to make a peace poster. Examples: arms joined, a gun turning into a dove, arms of students linked across an outline of the shape of your country, etc.

End with the Peaceful Star Relaxation exercise.

PEACE LESSON 13

Peace Slogans

Play a peace song as the class begins.
Discuss the Reflection Point:

♦ "Peace must begin with each one of us. Through quiet and
serious reflection on its meaning, new and creative ways
can be found to foster understanding, friendships and
cooperation among all peoples."
—*Javier Perez de Cuellar,*
Former Secretary-General of the United Nations

Activity

Ask the students if they have thought of any other peace slogans. Provide the materials for painting their slogans on pieces
of paper. Their work could initially decorate the room. Later,
during a school assembly, posters and slogans could be moved
to the larger gathering place.

Admire the peace slogans around the room.

End with a relaxation exercise.

PEACE LESSON 14

Remembering War

Choose subject content: Teachers at West Kidlington School
used Remembrance Day poems about war as the content for the
discussion. Choose something relevant in your curriculum.

Discuss/Share

The language and feelings in the poems—or whatever content you have chosen. Then ask:

- What are the causes of war? (often desire for power, wealth and territory)
- What happens to people when there is war?
- Find war-torn countries in the atlas (two for younger students, more for older students).
- How do you feel about other people fighting?
- What does peace in your country mean to you?

Activity

Write a poem in any style on your own thoughts about war and/or peace.

—Contributed by West Kidlington School

NOTE TO TEACHER PRIOR TO LESSON 15

Conflict Resolution

If students are not resolving conflicts in an optimum manner, conflict resolution strategies might be considered for the class or the entire school. Lessons in conflict resolution are simple, develop good communication skills which are useful in life and have proved to be successful. There are many excellent resources, each one varying to some degree. In some schools, students serve as peer conflict resolution managers during break and playtime. The students often wear a special sash, cap or armband to identify their role.

Peace

The Conflict Resolution Process: First, the students in conflict are asked if they want help in resolving the problem. If they do, one or two conflict managers sit with them. One can sit by one upset student, the other by the other upset student. It is more comfortable for two conflict managers to be together so they can give each other moral support. If one or both students say they do not want help and they are not willing to listen and talk, then they are both sent to the school office, to the supervising adult or to whomever the usual disciplinary procedure identifies.

The "conflict resolution managers" or "peer mediators" are there to help the students solve the conflict. They listen to their replies and direct them to listen to each other rather than interrupting. The peer mediators encourage the students to listen carefully without interruption and then repeat to each other what they heard the other say. Their job is to appreciate the disputants' listening and problem-solving skills and to avoid taking sides. They are not to blame, accuse, moralize or judge. They are there to help the students resolve the conflict. It is easy to slip into old verbal patterns, so be careful!

- A conflict resolution manager starts with the more visibly upset student, asking him or her to state what happened.

- Ask the second student to listen and repeat back what he or she heard. (He or she is not to contradict, argue or blame, but simply repeat.)

- The same question—what happened?—is then posed to the second student, and the first student listens carefully and repeats.

- The next question asked each student is, "How were you feeling?"

- Again, each listens and repeats what the other said.

Peace

- Next, they are asked what they would like to stop happening.

- After they each answer and have repeated back what the other said, then they are asked what they would like to happen instead.

- The students are then asked if they can agree to do what the other suggested.

- If they are not happy with that suggestion, they are asked to generate other solutions.

- They are then asked if they can make a firm commitment to try to behave in the way they both agreed.

- When both have agreed to another behavior, the conflict resolution managers compliment them and tell them to return to the regular school activity.

Starting Up Conflict Resolution in Schools: All students are taught the same communication process. Tell the students about the process, demonstrate it for them and lead them in practice. One person may want to visit the different classes and do all the training, or teachers can be taught how to do this at a teacher training session. Post the conflict resolution questions/process in each classroom. These are listed in the summarizing steps below and are also contained in the Appendix, Item 3.

Conflict resolution managers might want to take the questions with them to the playground and even take notes during the process. Let all students know that if they have a conflict on the playground, they may go to the student conflict resolution managers, or other students can call the managers to come over. As part of giving the students more ownership in this process, you may wish to have a contest for renaming the conflict resolution managers. Perhaps you would get suggestions to call them peacemakers, stars, or ? The students could submit possible names, and there could be a schoolwide selection of the name.

Conflict resolution has had dramatic effects in teaching students how to mediate disagreements and fights. Several teams of students can rotate as conflict resolution managers. Adults should positively comment on the courage and qualities of the students—both of the conflict resolution managers and of the students who are willing to communicate and listen to help resolve a problem.

Conflict Resolution Process: Summary of Steps

The mediator asks each student the question:

Are you willing to work on a solution? If the answer is "yes," continue.

Ask each student one question at a time, waiting for his or her response.

The other student listens and repeats what was said.

Please tell us what happened.

How did you feel when that happened?

What would you like to stop?

What would you like him or her to do instead?

Can you do that?

Can you make a firm commitment to try to behave in the way you both have agreed?

Compliment them for the qualities they showed during this peace process.

Peace

Conflict Resolution

Teacher preparation: Be familiar with the above information, and list the questions used during conflict resolution on a poster or board.

Are you willing to work on a solution?

Each person has to be willing to LISTEN to the other and repeat what the other says. Please tell us what happened.

How did you feel when that happened?

What would you like to stop?

What would you like him or her to do instead?

Can you do that?

Can you commit to trying to behave in the way you two have agreed?

Begin the session with a peace song.

Ask: "What would happen in the world if everyone learned to communicate and solve problems instead of fighting?"

Acknowledge their responses.

Say, "People all over the world are learning about conflict resolution. The more people learn it, the more there is hope for peace. I really believe that people can solve their problems."

Say, "Today we're going to learn one method of conflict resolution. These are the steps." Review the steps you have written on a poster or board.

Go back to the first question and the sentence under it. Ask:

- Willingness to work on a problem really helps, doesn't it? Why?
- What does it mean about you as a person if you are willing to work on a problem? (If they have not included the following answers, please do include them: "It takes courage to work on a problem. It means that you believe you are capable of finding a solution, and it means you believe other people are capable, too.")

Say, "It's good to start with the problems we know about. Let's list them":

- What kinds of things do people your age fight over? Listen and list their responses. (In classes with older students, ask them to write the responses on the board.)
- How do you feel when _____ (one event mentioned) happens?
- If the feeling is anger, ask: What feeling is underneath that feeling?
- How do you feel when _____ (another event mentioned) happens?
- If the feeling is anger, ask: What feeling is underneath that feeling?
- How do you want to feel? Accept all responses. Ask them if they want to feel valued, respected and loved (if they have not given those responses).

Peace

Demonstration: Ask for two volunteers to try the conflict resolution exercise. Let them pretend to have a common conflict or else enact a recent conflict. The teacher models asking each student the questions and asks them to listen to each other.

NOTE TO TEACHER

Actively listen to their replies, direct them to listen to each other and repeat what the other says. Appreciate their listening and coming up with solutions. If a student blames, interrupts or accuses the other during the dialogue, say "Please listen," or "Please answer the question," and restate the question again: "How did you feel when that happened?"

Ask for two more volunteers and demonstrate the conflict resolution process again. Thank the volunteers. Ask for questions or reactions.

The students may want to learn the peace rap song "Cool Off" (in the Appendix) or make up their own song.

End with a Relaxation exercise.

Lesson

16

PEACE LESSON 16

What We Like and Don't Like— Under the Anger

Begin with a peace song.

Peace

Discussion: Say, "Yesterday we were discussing some of the things people have conflicts over and we made a list of those. Let's look at them in relation to the questions asked during the conflict resolution process."

Take one item from the list, for example, name-calling, and ask the following questions:

- How do you feel when that happens? (If the response is anger, ask: What feeling is underneath that?)
- What would you like the other person(s) to stop doing?
- What would you like the other person(s) to do/say instead?

Repeat the above process with another couple of items from the list.

Say, "In some ways, people are simple. When we get angry, there is hurt or fear or embarrassment underneath. The hurt and fear come first when people do not feel valued, respected or loved. Some people stay feeling hurt and others handle it by getting angry." Repeat what you just said and illustrate it on the board, drawing flames above the word "anger."

Anger
Everyone wants to be valued, respected or loved.
Hurt or Fear or Embarrassment

Apply concept: Ask the students to think of examples of things that happen or a time they felt this way when something happened to them. If they are unable think of an example, use examples from the list of conflicts made previously.

Activity

Instruct the students to form pairs or small groups and ask them to create a poster on what others should not do or what behaviors they would like from others. The students may need another day to finish their posters and have those who wish to share do so.

PEACE LESSON 17

Conflict Resolution and Listening

Begin with a peace song.

Demonstrate the conflict resolution process one time with a couple of volunteers.

Discuss/Share

Say, "One of the most important things in solving problems is to listen to others and really hear what they have to say." Ask:

- How do you feel when you try to talk to someone and he or she turns away?

Acknowledge: "Yes, when people don't listen and are rude, problems usually get worse."

"Sometimes people do other things that interfere with solving a problem." Ask: "Would anybody like to guess what some of those things could be?" Acknowledge their responses and add any of the following not mentioned.

Blaming

Telling the person he or she is silly or stupid

Interrupting

Accusing

Contradicting ("Wait your turn, and listen. This one takes patience and respect!")

Trying to make him or her feel guilty

Getting angry because the other person is angry

Explain: "For effective listening, it is important to do two things":

1. To really (genuinely) pay attention to what the person is saying, and
2. To let the other person know that you understand what he or she is saying.

Listening Activity

Form groups of three students. Ask them to count off one, two and three. For Round One: Person One will be the Talker, Person Two the Listener and Person Three the Observer. See the chart below.

	Person One	**Person Two**	**Person Three**
Round One	Talker	Listener	Observer
Round Two	Observer	Talker	Listener
Round Three	Listener	Observer	Talker

- For Rounds One, Two and Three, each Talker shares something positive that happened to him or her.

Peace

- Do the rounds again, this time asking each Talker to share something that is important to him or her or something that makes him or her feel peaceful.
- Do the rounds again, this time asking each Talker to share something that he or she feels angry or sad about. (If there is not sufficient time, continue this activity during the next lesson.)

During each round, the Listener should be encouraged to listen, occasionally reflecting the feelings or emotions of the Talker, or restating or paraphrasing the content of the message. The Observer in each round can provide feedback.

Discuss/Share

- How did you feel when someone really listened to you?
- Did anyone notice that anger automatically started to decrease when the person was genuinely listened to?

Say, "Real listening is giving respect. People who listen well have self-respect."

End with a Relaxation exercise.

Options: A Peace Circle and/or a Peace Club

A Peace Circle can be a regular time once a day or once a week when students and the teacher name actions they saw during the day or week that contributed to peace. It is also a wonderful idea when there is a conflict in the classroom or when students come into the classroom with an unresolved conflict. A Peace Circle can be "called into session" as needed. It is wise for the teacher to be the mediator of a real conflict in the classroom. While it may seem to some teachers that this would take time away from teaching, most teachers who try it report that dealing with the conflict ends up saving time. Students learn that real conflicts are very solvable. Additionally, the teacher is demonstrating that peace is important to him or her—and so are the feelings of the students. When there is harmony, it is much easier to feel and do our best.

Students and a teacher who is willing to be an advisor can set up a Peace Club. Students can create their own activities. Peer mediators could continue to refine and practice their methods with the help of the advisor as well as share with other mediators. Members of the Peace Club could create assemblies and dramas, create messages of peace, give Peace Awards and acknowledge others.

PEACE LESSON 18

Conflict Resolution—Peers as Mediators

Begin with a peace song.
Discuss the Reflection Points:

♦ Peace begins with each one of us.
♦ To stay peaceful requires strength and compassion.

Activity

Ask four students to volunteer for a conflict resolution demonstration. Two act as mediators and two pretend to have a conflict.

Peace

The peer mediators will take over the role the teacher had been playing in asking the questions and helping the students in conflict resolve the problem. Instruct each peer mediator to sit by the students who have the conflict. When one demonstration is finished, ask the four students to reverse roles.

Note: There is a conflict resolution sheet for the mediators to use in the Appendix.

Contrast poetry activity: If time remains, ask students to brainstorm vocabulary associated with the above activities. They can use a dictionary and thesaurus to find synonyms and antonyms. As a group, or as individuals, students can write poetry to take the reader from one feeling or idea to its opposite. The point is to use words to show a change in feelings as a conflict is resolved. For example:

Anger

Hot resistance

Eyes bright, throat too tight

Nails digging deep into fists

Itching to fight

Eyes meet

A tear trickles down an inflamed check

"I'm sorry"

"Me too"

Acceptance

—Contributed by Ruth Liddle

Homework assignment: Ask the students to do interviews during the next couple of days with adults. Review the following assignments.

PEACE LESSONS 19 AND 20

Interviews

Lessons 19-20

Begin with a peace song.

Eight to Eleven Activity: In the next couple of days, interview two adults to find out what peace means to them and how they find peace in their lives. Start off by asking each person to complete these sentences for you:

Peace is . . .

If I want to feel relaxed and peaceful, I . . .

The most peaceful place I can remember is . . .

Twelve to Fourteen Activity: Gather information from the television, radio news, newspapers or magazines about a couple of wars. Talk with an adult about what the people are fighting over. Ask yourself, *"Is there an alternative to fighting?"* Write down your thoughts. Now ask this question to at least two adults and write down what they say.

Ask the students to share the results of their interviews in class.

—*Contributed by Ruth Liddle*

PEACE LESSON 21

Peaceful Colors, Angry Colors

Lesson 21

Choose subject content: Your country may have a holiday remembering veterans of war, or you may wish to use as subject

Peace

content a violent event that the students know of or are concerned about.

Discuss/Share

Talk about the subject content. Ask the students about the process involved within the content (as in the following questions), and then perhaps share some of your thoughts.

How can feelings escalate so that small upsets become big and out of control?

- How can we try and control these angry feelings and replace them by calmer, peaceful ones? (the help of friends, etc.).
- How does being at peace with oneself and one's friends make for a happier life?

Activity

Draw or paint peaceful and angry colors and shapes—peaceful on one half of the paper, angry on the other half.

—Contributed by Linda Heppenstall

PEACE LESSON 22

Contrast and Solve

Begin with a Relaxation exercise.
Discuss the Reflection Points:

♦ Peace begins within each one of us.

Peace

♦ If everyone in the world were peaceful, this would be a peaceful world.

Ask

- What allows the negative to continue to grow?
- What types of thoughts keep conflict alive?
- What allows peace to grow?
- What types of thoughts help peace grow?

Activity

Create different stories. Instruct the students to start with a peaceful situation that changes to a negative situation. Then start with a negative situation that changes to a positive one. Find original ways to transform/solve the negative situations. The class may wish to create a reference book on solutions the students have found.

Eight to Ten Variation: This could be done as a continuous verbal story. The students create the story themselves, with one person starting, the next continuing, etc.

Eleven to Fourteen Activity: Depending on time, you may want students to create a verbal story as above, or small groups could create and enact plays. After each play, ask the students to comment on what gestures convey negativity or aggressiveness and what gestures convey peace.

—Contributed by Sabine Levy and Pilar Quera Colomina

Peace

PEACE LESSON 23

Peace Heroes

Discuss the Reflection Point: To stay peaceful requires strength and compassion.

Eight to Eleven Activity: Write a story on "The Peace Hero." Divide the class into small groups. Allow the students to read their stories to each other. The group can then decide which story they would like to act out for the class.

—*Contributed by Marcia Maria Lins de Medeiros*

Twelve to Fourteen Activity: Study peace heroes of your culture(s). Make up a skit about them or share what interests you about their beliefs or methods.

PEACE LESSON 24

Collaborative Painting

Play a peace song.

Discuss/Share

Ask the students what they enjoyed about the unit on peace and what they learned. Admire the work around the room and their accomplishments.

Eight to Ten Activity: Discuss what the students would like to put on their collaborative painting—symbols of peace, Peace

Peace

Star, a picture of a peaceful world? Provide students with a long piece of colorful paper and individual small pots of paint and a brush. Play peaceful music. As they stand close to each other, they can paint their own small planned pattern. When the music stops, each student moves one step to the left or right.

—Contributed by Linda Heppenstall

Eleven to Fourteen Activity: Divide the class into five groups of students. Each group is responsible for painting the sky, earth, buildings, people and animals. Provide students with a long piece of paper and enough individual small pots of paint and brushes for two groups. Play peaceful music and begin the Imagining a Peaceful World exercise from Lesson 1. Start to read the visualization very slowly. Each group can get up in turn to draw and paint its part of the picture. One person from each group can add to the visualization—adding verbal commentaries that include descriptions of what the group is painting. Everyone should have a good time while enjoying the music and staying in a state of peace. (This is intended as an experience, not a polished piece of art!)

Additional Peace Activities

Dance peace.

Write your advice to the adults of the world. Make a class book for the adults who visit to read. Or send the books to adults in decision-making positions.

Peace

Additional Peace Activity for Students Ages 8–11

Dove Game

Discuss the following Peace Point: Peace begins within each one of us.

Activity

Make squares for the Dove Game or for an adaptation of a children's board game in your country. The Dove Game is an adaptation of a game from Spain called the Goose Game. The Spanish board game has squares that form a spiral. Small groups of students can make the board game, drawing objects on small pieces of paper that can be later pasted onto a larger piece of paper in the form of a spiral. Or each member of the entire class can make one square, and then the squares can be laid on the floor of the classroom or outside in a large spiral. In the former, students would use dice and markers when they play. In the latter, they would use dice, but then stand by the square on the ground as they advance toward the finish.

Discuss/Share

Ask the students to think about what pictures they would like to make for their game. There should be doves and other symbols of peace. One out of every five pictures should be a dove. Two out of every five pictures can be something that disrupts peace. For these, ask the students to draw pictures about what things they do not like other people to do. Arrange the pictures so that the fifth square is a dove, and then the tenth, fifteenth, twentieth, etc. The last picture should be a picture of a completely peaceful world.

Game Rules: To play, the student rolls the dice. When a student lands on a picture of a dove, he or she says, "Dove to dove, I fly above," and then moves to the next dove (five spaces up). If a student lands on a disrupting-peace square, he or she gives a solution. For example, if it is a picture of someone calling a name, the student can say, "I don't like it when you do that; I want you to stop." Or if it is a picture of someone gossiping, he or she can say, "I feel _____ when you talk about me because _____." When a student thinks of a solution, he or she advances to the next peace square. The game is over when everyone reaches the last square of a peaceful world. Allow the students to encourage and help each other. The teacher can lead the applause when everyone reaches the last square.

—Adapted from an activity contributed by Encarnación Royo Costa

Activity

Play the Dove Game made in the previous lesson. First explain the rules, then ask the students to practice verbal responses in preparation for landing on the dove and conflict squares. Then ask them to play the game.

End with a peace song.

Peace

Additional Peace Lessons for Students Ages 12–14

Manifestations of Peace in the World

What are different manifestations of peace in the world? How is peace expressed through the arts? What large organizations work for peace in the world? In different subject areas, use your standard curriculum for students to explore. This will require the student participation in researching information and sharing it with the class. They could create a paper on this theme.

—*Contributed by Sabine Levy and Pilar Quera Colomina*

TWO

Respect

2. RESPECT UNIT

Respect

Respect Reflection Points

◆ The first respect is to respect myself—to know that I am naturally valuable.

◆ Part of self-respect is knowing my own qualities.

◆ Respect is knowing I am unique and valuable.

◆ Respect is knowing I am lovable and capable.

◆ Respect is listening to others.

◆ Respect is knowing others are valuable, too.

◆ Respect for the self is the seed that gives growth to confidence.

◆ When we have respect for ourselves, it is easy to have respect for others.

◆ Those who show respect will receive respect.

◆ To know one's worth and to honor the worth of others is how one earns respect.

◆ Everyone in the world has the right to live with respect and dignity, including myself.

◆ Part of respect is knowing I make a difference.

Respect

Respect Unit

GOAL: To think about and experience self-respect.
OBJECTIVES:

❑ To state and be able to discuss two Respect Reflection Points about respect for the self.

❑ To identify times when they have a feeling of respect for the self.

❑ To identify five qualities of the self.

❑ To enjoy the Respect Relaxation exercises by the end of the unit, as demonstrated by sitting quietly during it and appearing content to do so.

❑ To make a tree of their qualities and related successes.

❑ To paint respect or be part of a dance portraying respect.

GOAL: To increase knowledge about respect.
OBJECTIVES:

❑ To state and talk about two Respect Reflection Points on respect for others.

❑ To participate in a discussion about feelings when people show respect and disrespect.

❑ To identify how people show respect and disrespect.

❑ To write a few lines of advice on how people should treat each other.

❑ To learn several greetings or polite phrases in other languages.

❑ To identify different ways to show respect to adults.

❑ To write a story or cartoon on respecting the environment.

Respect

GOAL: To build respect relationship skills.

OBJECTIVES:

❑ To identify five qualities that they admire in others.

❑ To write down one positive quality for each student participating in the Your Qualities activity.

❑ During a conflict resolution discussion, to be able to generate an alternative respectful behavior that would help solve the problem.

❑ To learn the response, "I don't like it when you call me names. I want you to stop," and to be able to apply that response or another appropriate response if the situation arises.

❑ For students ten and older, to be able to fill in the blanks to the problem-solving communication skill: "I feel _____ _____ when you _____ because _____."

❑ To show respect to others by listening when they are speaking, as demonstrated by being able to listen to others during the values discussion time.

❑ To understand how each person can make a positive difference, as demonstrated through his or her story, interview or slogan.

❑ To develop problem-solving skills as demonstrated by discussing various sensible solutions to the Situation Cards.

Respect Lessons

 Add to the above list of Reflection Points, using favorite sayings from your culture, sayings from legends or quotes from respected individuals.

Respect

Play a song every day as "values time" begins. You may want to teach traditional songs or ask students to bring songs that relate to the theme. Students may want to make up their own respect points or slogans.

RESPECT LESSON 1

Qualities

Explain that in the next few weeks the school/class will be exploring respect.

Discuss/Share

- Who can tell me about respect?
- Why is respect important?

Discuss the following Reflection Points:

♦ The first respect is to respect myself—to know that I am naturally valuable.
♦ Part of self-respect is knowing my own qualities.

Ask:

- When do you feel good about yourself?
- When do you have a feeling of respect for yourself?

Students will sometimes mention specific things they do that are helpful to others as a time when they feel good about themselves. Confirm that when we do good things we feel good about ourselves. They will often mention a time when they look pretty

Respect

or handsome or have something new. Accept and acknowledge all responses.

Activity

Say, "Today we are going to look at our own personal qualities, the things that are good about us. We all have many things that are the same, but one of the great things about humans is that each has a personality of his or her own. Each person comes with a unique combination of qualities. Let's start by listing good qualities that people can have." Ask:

- What qualities do you admire in your friends?
- Think about someone you admire. What qualities do you admire in that person?
- Think about your heroes. What qualities do they have that you like?

Say, "It is said that any quality you admire is really yours."

The teacher can lead the students in brainstorming personal qualities, such as friendly, loyal, sweet, kind and compassionate. Depending on the vocabulary of the students, you may want to include creative, gentle, witty, cooperative, confident, humble, loyal, trustworthy, industrious, benevolent, diligent, artistic, generous, economical, sensible, sweet, loving, caring, patient and/or tolerant. Keep the list of qualities you create together on the board.

Ask the students to think about these qualities and then write down five or more qualities they know they have.

Say, "Now write down a few times when you felt really good about yourself. Just write one line to remind yourself of that time." (Give them several minutes to do this.) "Now I want you to think of the quality that you showed you had on each one of those times." (Give them several more minutes.) Give a few examples if they need it, such as: "If you remember a time when you helped someone, you might put down loving, caring or compassionate. If you remember a time you returned something to someone who lost it, you might put honest."

Instruct them to add those qualities to their list of qualities.

Eight to Nine Activity: Instruct the students to draw a picture of a time they felt full of respect. They can add their qualities to the picture, writing, "I am _____."

RESPECT LESSON 2

Story

Read "Lily the Leopard" (Appendix) to the students ages eight and nine or another story that you like on respect. For older students, select another story from your culture or curriculum on the theme of respect or disrespect.

Mention the following Reflection Point in relation to the story: "Respect is knowing I am unique and valuable. Lily knew she was unique, but at first she did not realize she was valuable."

Discuss the story read. The first two of the following questions are for the story, "Lily the Leopard." The other questions can be used with many stories.

- Why did they treat Lily (or the person from another story) without respect? (Lily was different.)

- How did Lily (or the person from another story) feel when the others were mean?
- How did the characters show disrespect?
- How could the other characters in the story have shown respect?
- How do people your age sometimes show disrespect? What types of things do they do?
- How do you feel when that happens to you?
- How do you feel when that happens to other people?
- How do people show respect?
- Why do people sometimes not act respectfully?

Mention if they have not: "Sometimes kids who act with disrespect don't know better. Maybe someone older treated them with disrespect. However, people who show disrespect don't have real respect inside."

Say, "One of the Reflection Points is: Those who show respect will receive respect." Ask:

- Can you think of examples of that?
- What would be your advice to people who show disrespect?
- How would you like people to treat each other?

Eight to Eleven Activity: Instruct the students to write a few lines of advice about how people should treat each other. They may wish to share their sentences with the class.

Younger students may enjoy illustrating their advice with a picture.

Twelve to Fourteen Activity: Discuss in small groups how you would like people to treat each other. Write your advice on a poster and present it to the class.

Respect

RESPECT LESSON 3

Your Qualities

Begin with a song.

Activity

Make sure the list of qualities generated during the first Respect lesson is in plain view. Pass out paper to everyone. Ask each student to write his or her name at the top of the paper. The objective is for students to pass around the paper, each writing the quality he or she sees in the person whose name is at the top. Everyone's paper should be passed to everyone else before being returned to the rightful owner. Allow the students to read their list of qualities for a minute before continuing.

Introduce the Garden Image Relaxation/Focusing exercise: Say, "Relaxation/Focusing exercises are one way to enjoy and strengthen the feeling of respect inside. The one we are going to do today uses the image of a garden. Perhaps later one of you would like to make up one using the image of an ocean or another image."

Garden Image Relaxation/Focusing Exercise

"Sit comfortably and let your body relax. . . . As you breathe slowly, let your mind be still and calm. . . . Starting at your feet, let yourself relax. . . . Relax your legs . . . your stomach . . . your shoulders . . . your neck . . . your face . . . your nose . . . your eyes . . . and your forehead. . . . Your mind is serene and calm. . . .

Respect

Breathe deeply. . . . Concentrate on stillness. . . . In your mind, picture a flower. . . . Imagine the smell. . . . Enjoy its fragrance. . . . Observe its shape and color. . . . Enjoy its beauty. . . . Each person is like a flower. . . . Each one of us is unique . . . yet we have many things in common. . . . Picture a garden around you with many varieties of flowers . . . all of them beautiful. . . . Each flower with its color . . . each flower with its fragrance. . . giving the best of itself. . . . Some are tall with pointed petals, some with rounded petals, some are big and others little. . . . Some have many hues of colors. . . . Some attract the eye because of their simplicity. . . . Each one of us is like a beautiful flower. . . . Enjoy the beauty of each one. . . . Each adds beauty to the garden. . . . All are important. . . . Together they form the garden. . . . Each flower has respect for itself. . . . When one respects oneself, it is then easy to respect others. . . . Each one is valuable and unique. . . . With respect, the qualities of others are seen. . . . Perceive what is good in each one. . . . Each has a unique role. . . . Each is important. . . . Let this image fade in your mind, and turn your attention to this room again."

—Contributed by Amadeo Dieste Castejon

 Discuss the Reflection Point: Respect for the self is the seed that gives growth to confidence.

Lessons
4-8

RESPECT LESSONS 4 THROUGH 8

Colors of Respect and Disrespect and Me Mobiles

Begin each day with a song.

Respect

Respect Lesson 4

Announce to the students that you are going to explore the effects of respect and disrespect. "In the next couple days we're going to experiment with respect. I'm going to give half of you these strips of green paper to wear around your upper arms, and half of you purple strips to wear around your upper arms." Tell them in this experiment a "pretend" government has declared the green group to be the elite group. Elite means the best. The government notices that the greens have a disrespectful attitude toward the purples.

Activity

For a limited time period (perhaps one period in middle school or half of the morning in primary school), instruct the green group to only show respect to other greens, while being disrespectful (in attitude, not words) to the purples. At the end of the session, remind them that this was for the purpose of exploring the topic of respect and disrespect. Inform them that tomorrow the government will be changing!

Allow the students to make Me Mobiles for three sessions as they do the "Colors of Respect and Disrespect" exercise.

Me Mobiles

Say, "Part of learning to have respect for yourself is knowing your qualities and knowing yourself. This week, our art project is making a mobile about yourself. You can use your creativity. Over here there is string, paper, colored pens, colored paper and little sticks. You can bring in tin cans or cartons to hang, and decorate them with colored paper. Each object on the mobile is to represent an aspect of you."

- Favorite pastimes
- Your qualities
- Your family
- What you like about nature
- Your favorite animals
- How you give to others
- What you believe in
- Your favorite food

List the above categories on the board.

Ask: "Does anyone have another area to add?"

Review the list. Do this slowly for younger students so they have time to think about their answers in each area. Circulate among the students as they work on the mobile, listen and positively affirm their output.

An easy way to construct the mobile is to tie two sticks together in an **X** and then hang objects from the ends of the sticks at different lengths. Students can use three sticks if they wish. A string from the middle—where the two or three sticks are tied—then goes to the ceiling. A coat hanger may be used instead of the sticks.

Respect Lesson 5

Reverse the students' roles the next period, or the next day if you have the students for only one period. ("The government has now changed hands and the purples are the elite.") Follow this with a class discussion on the students' feelings and perceptions.

Discuss/Share

- How did they feel as the elite?
- How did it feel to be the "non-elite?"
- Would they like a world in which everyone has respect for all?
- How would the world be different?

Respect Lesson 6

The next session, distribute a whole rainbow of colored armbands. Now they are all princes and princesses from different kingdoms! Ask the students to give regard to everyone through their looks, attitudes and behavior. Discuss feelings and perceptions.

At the end of the session, do the following Relaxation/Focusing exercise.

Star of Respect Exercise

"Let's think of the stars and imagine ourselves to be just like them. They are so beautiful in the sky, and they sparkle and shine. . . . They are so quiet and peaceful. . . . Be very still. . . . Relax your toes and legs. . . . Relax your stomach . . . and your shoulders. . . . Relax your arms . . . and your face. . . . Feel safe . . . and allow a soft light of peace to surround you. . . . Inside you are like a beautiful little star. . . . You are lovable and capable. . . . You are who you are. . . . Each person brings special qualities to the world. . . . You are valuable. . . . Enjoy the feeling of respect inside. . . . You are stars of respect. . . . Let yourself be quiet and peaceful inside. . . . Focus. . . . You are concentrated . . . full of respect . . . content. . . . Slowly bring your attention back to the room."

Respect

Respect Lesson 7

Students continue to wear the variety of armbands. However, tell them that blue means they have the best education, green means they are hard workers, purple means they have a good sense of humor, etc. End the activity with a discussion.

- What does this group (and all of humanity) have in common? (All are human beings, each one has something to offer, etc.)

Activity

Ask the students to write a short personal essay on their experience. How did they feel when receiving disrespect, how did they feel when receiving respect, how did they feel when everyone was a prince or princess?

Respect Lesson 8

Activity

Instruct the students to write a poem or song or to draw a picture. Ask them to express their feelings about and reactions to any part of the Colors of Respect experiment. Share these in class.

End with the Respect Relaxation exercise.

Respect

RESPECT LESSON 9
Stories

Read stories about people who learn to have self-respect or who maintain their self-respect. Ask older students to bring in their favorite stories, including real stories from the newspaper. Or investigate real stories of your culture's heroes.

RESPECT LESSON 10
Greetings of the World

Begin with the Peace Relaxation exercise.

Introduction: One way of showing respect to others is learning about their culture and learning to say things in their language. Learn about different ways around the world of greeting others with respect.

Activity

Depending on the age group and language skills of the class, learn several greetings and polite phrases in two to four languages. Perhaps students in the class have a variety of languages to share and can share gestures or a dance. Enjoy practicing.

—Contributed by Dominique Ache

Respect

RESPECT LESSON 11
Two Birds

Practice the greetings and phrases in the different languages from the last lesson.

Read the story, "Two Birds," in the Appendix, or read another story about a person taking offense because of a difference of opinion.

Discuss/Share

- Why did the bird get upset?
- What did the other bird say that made it worse?
- Do you ever feel insulted?
- What did both birds find out? (Each one was seeing the leaves from his own perspective; hence, what each one saw was correct from his point of view.)
- What can we learn from this story?
- How could the birds have responded differently so that they weren't ready to fight?

—*Contributed by Sabine Levy and Pilar Quera Colomina*

Activity

Ask six students to volunteer to come to the front of the class and stand in a row. Give a pencil to the first student and ask her or him to hand it to the next student and so on down the row. Then, give the pencil to the first student again, and ask all the students in the line to hand it to each other with respect. Ask:

Respect

- Was there a difference in the way the pencil was being given?
- What was different?
- Did you feel differently when it was being given with lots of respect? How?

RESPECT LESSON 12

Strategies to Stop Conflict

Lesson 12

Begin with a song.

Bring out the list of things students fight about that the teacher and class made during Peace Lesson 15.

Introduction: Say, "Very often conflict occurs when someone shows disrespect to someone else. Today we're going to take a look at the list we made when we were exploring Peace of the things people do that cause conflicts and fights. Sometimes when people do the things that are on this list, we get hurt or angry. We feel bad when people treat us without respect. But always remember that you define who you are. You are the one that knows your qualities. If someone calls you 'stupid,' does that mean you are stupid? No. Every single one of you is a valuable and worthwhile human being. Okay, let's look at this list in the light of respect."

Discuss/Share

Take one item on the list, and ask:

- Would this have occurred if the person were showing respect?

Respect

- What would you like or advise this person to do instead? What would have been a better way to handle it?
- Would the problem have occurred then?
- If the person this was done to maintained self-respect, how could he or she handle it differently so the problem does not build?

Help the class problem-solve. See what alternatives they generate. Let them know when they come up with a good idea.

If someone offers an idea that is hurtful to someone, ask what the consequences might be of that action. Allow the students to supply the answers.

Ask them to come up with several ways to handle the situation. Help them create sensible strategies. For example:

- Ages eight to nine: When someone does something you don't like (like call a name), one thing you can do is tell him or her, "I don't like it when you to call me names. I'd like you to stop." Ask the class to repeat that several times with you, and then ask them to pair up and practice saying that in self-respect (firmly, clearly, but not aggressively).
- Ages nine through fourteen: Ask the students to generate clear and assertive things they can say instead of "I don't like it when you call me names . . ." Perhaps, "Hey, it's not cool to do that," "I'm not into fighting," or (to a friend), "Are you angry today? What's the matter?" Let them pair up and practice saying that in self-respect.
- Teach the following formula. This is a good idea to use when somebody you know does something you do not like (such as gossiping, name calling, etc.). "I feel _____

_____ when you _____

because _____

_____."

Give a couple of examples, such as:

"I feel bad when you talk to me about Marsha that way because she is my friend. I like you and I like Marsha, too. I think it's okay to like both of you."

"I feel pressured when you keep asking me to smoke because I already told you I don't want to do that. I know what I want to do, and I want you to respect that."

Ask students to create "I feel" strategies for each situation they bring up.

Note: The "I feel" communication skill may be a little difficult for eight- and nine-year-olds. If necessary, begin by helping them identify their feelings, such as happy, angry, sad or hurt.

Take several more items from the list made during Peace Lesson 15 and ask the same four questions above, helping the students develop strategies.

Discuss the following Reflection Point: When we have respect for ourselves, it is easy to have respect for others.

Follow-up: Ask the students to use the above "I feel _____

_____."

formula and fill in the blanks for two situations.

Respect

RESPECT LESSON 13

A Tree

Activity

Each student can make a tree, writing his or her personal qualities and talents in the roots, the positive things he or she does in the branches, and successes of those things in the leaves and fruits. The trees could be drawn on paper or made of other available materials. Each student could share his or her drawing in a group of four, while the other students listen with respect and perhaps add things the creator had not included.

—Contributed by Sabine Levy and Pilar Quera Colomina

RESPECT LESSON 14

Different Ways of Showing Respect

Discuss these Reflection Points and ask the following questions:

♦ Respect is knowing others are valuable, too.
♦ To know one's worth and to honor the worth of others is how one earns respect.

Ask:

• What are the different ways we show respect to adults?
• What are the different ways we show respect to nature?
• What are the different ways we show respect to objects?

Respect

- What are the different ways we show respect to common spaces?
- What can we do to make sure respect is given?

Ask the students to divide into groups to analyze each topic and make suggestions. They may wish to make explanatory posters.

—Contributed by Sabine Levy and Pilar Quera Colomina

End with the Respect Relaxation Exercise.

Note: The teacher may wish to give the students another day to share their answers with the class and finish their posters.

RESPECT LESSON 15

Respect for Friends

Lesson

15

Discuss the Reflection Point: Everyone in the world has the right to live with respect and dignity, including me.

Activity

Create a cartoon or a story on respect for friends, or write an essay.

—Contributed by Marcia Maria Lins de Medeiros

Respect

RESPECT LESSON 16

Situation Cards

The Situation Cards provide students with the opportunity to discuss various alternatives in dealing with real-life situations. You will find the cards in the Appendix. The teacher may wish to photocopy the situation cards or let students copy them onto card stock.

Many classes really enjoy this activity, as it provides a forum for students to discuss their real concerns and apply the practical skills they have been learning through the values activities. The teacher acts as a facilitator. Avoid moralizing and telling them what they "should" do (sometimes this is difficult). Instead, listen and encourage them to respond. Ask them the consequences, both positive and negative, when their answers are appropriate and inappropriate. They will end up teaching themselves and each other. If their answers continue to be inappropriate, ask them how they would feel if they were the other person. Ask them to role-play the situation and then exchange roles. Ask the class if a "fair" solution has been generated.

Activity

Read a Situation Card to the class and encourage them to generate responses. Ask:

- How could you use the value of peace?
- What could you do?
- What do you think would happen then?

- What else could you say or do?
- How could you use the value of respect?
- What could you do? (etc.)

Read another Situation Card or two and enjoy the class discussion. The next time you do Situation Cards, you may wish to allow students to form small groups. Identical Situation Cards could be given to each group. The students can take turns reading the cards and giving oral responses to the situations. If one group find a situation difficult, the class could share their solutions and discuss it as a whole group.

Extension Activities: Students could make up their own Situation Cards and later exchange them with other groups.

Students could act out the situations through role plays.

—Contributed by Trish Summerfield

End with a song.

RESPECT LESSON 17

Respect for the Environment

Activity

Create a cartoon or a story on respect for the environment. Share your creations.

Perhaps some of the students would like to create their own relaxation exercise using images from nature.

—Contributed by Marcia Maria Lins de Medeiros

Respect

Lesson 18

RESPECT LESSON 18
Making a Difference

Read the tale, "Fire in the Jungle," in the Appendix.

Discuss the Reflection Point: Part of respect is knowing I make a difference. Talk about the bird in the story in relationship to this point.

Perhaps the teacher would like to share a couple of positive stories about when he or she made a difference. Talk about the little things that make a difference—a smile, someone listening or believing in you. Ask the students to share a time when they made a difference in someone's life.

Activity

A follow-up activity could be drawing a scene from "Fire in the Jungle," making masks of animals and doing a skit, or making slogans which communicate that what we do makes a difference.

Homework: Interview a person at home or in the community. Ask the person to share about a time when someone had a positive impact on his or her life. Then ask the person to share about a positive difference he or she has made.

RESPECT LESSON 19
Making a Difference

Students ages eight and nine could orally share their stories. Another option is ask students to write a short story on the difference someone made in their life, how they made a difference for someone else, or a story on the person they interviewed.

Older students could also collect articles from newspapers on people who have made a positive difference.

RESPECT LESSON 20
Paint Respect

Discuss with the students what they have enjoyed and learned about respect.

Activity

Paint or dance Respect. Sing a Respect song. Do their favorite Relaxation exercise.

Respect

Lesson 21

RESPECT LESSON 21

A Skit on Respect

Students in the United Kingdom put on a skit at their school after doing this unit on Respect. They put up the word RESPECT in large letters, and then took up a topic for each letter. R for race, E for environment, S for self, P for property, E for emotions, C for caring for others, T for talents to develop. For younger students, help them make up a skit. For older students, divide the class into groups to make up their own.

—Contributed by Ann Stirzaker

THREE

Love

3. LOVE UNIT

73

Love

Love Reflection Points

♦ Everyone in this room is lovable and capable.

♦ When I am full of love, anger runs away.

♦ Love is the value that makes our relationships better.

♦ When my words give flowers instead of thorns, I create a better world.

♦ I can have love for myself, love for my family, love for others, love for my country, love for my goals and love for the world—all at the same time.

♦ Love for others means I want what is good for them.

♦ Love means I can be kind, caring and understanding.

♦ When we feel strong inside, it's easy to be loving.

♦ Love is caring, love is sharing.

♦ Love is being a trustworthy friend.

♦ "Our task must be to free ourselves . . . by widening our circle of compassion to embrace all living beings and all of nature." —Albert Einstein

♦ "The real law lives in the kindness of our hearts. If our hearts are empty, no law or political reform can fill them." —Tolstoy

Love

Love Unit

GOAL: To increase the experience of love.
OBJECTIVES:

- ❏ To think of kind ways to relate to the self.
- ❏ To think about widening their circle of compassion.
- ❏ To participate in a Relaxation/Focusing exercise on love.
- ❏ To create three of the following on the value of love: a story, song, dance, banner or poem.

GOAL: To increase knowledge about the effects of the values of love.
OBJECTIVES:

- ❏ To participate in discussions about the Love Reflection Points and be able to talk about three or more of them.
- ❏ To imagine a loving world and discuss the elements of that world.
- ❏ To identify what leaders/rulers in a loving world would want for the citizens.
- ❏ To think about and express their ideas about the components of a loving world and a non-loving world by making Mind Maps of each.
- ❏ To generate combined words to do with the quality of the heart and do a follow-up activity.
- ❏ To understand the importance of our words, i.e., "When my words give flowers instead of thorns, I create a better world."
- ❏ To identify loving and non-loving actions through discussions.

Love

GOAL: To exhibit fine social skills.

OBJECTIVES:

❏ To identify kind things to do and to carry out at least three of their ideas.

❏ To listen to a peer and to listen with appreciation to someone in their family.

❏ To generate ideas about appropriate or more loving behaviors during a conflict resolution exercise once the starting point of the negativity is identified.

Love Lessons

Occasionally include a Relaxation/Focusing exercise during "values time." You may wish to use those from the Peace and Respect units. The exercises are listed in the Appendix.

Songs

Play a song about love each morning as students are entering class or at the beginning of values time. Pick out some songs about love that students like. This will vary in different countries and with different languages. "Heal the World" by Michael Jackson is a good choice. Another choice is below.

The teacher may want to have the Love Reflection Point of the day already on the board so students can enter silently and reflect as they listen to the music.

Someday

	C F
Chorus:	Someday on the planet,

E min 7/C   D min 7/C   E min 7/C   D min 7/C   Emin7/ C

There will be perfect peace and harmony.

Eb   F/G   C

And all the people every where

Eb   F/G   C

Will love each other without fear.

Bb/F F   Bb/F   F

Verse 1:   I know the day is coming soon,

Ab/Eb   Eb   F

When there is no more hate,

Bb/F   F   Bb/F   F

And we see every one with love,

Ab/Eb   Eb   F

I know it's not too late.

Bb/F   F   Bb/F   F

Verse 2:   There won't be a need for guns,

Ab/Eb   Eb   F

And we'll have no more war.

Bb/F   F   Bb/F   F

And we can just play to-gether,

Ab/Eb   Eb   F

'Cause that's what life is for!

(Repeat chorus and verse 1)

Bb/F   F   Bb/F   F

Verse 3:   So let's talk our problems out,

Ab/Eb   Eb   F

Put our anger a-way.

Love

Bb/F   F   Bb/F   F

If we all can join to-gether,

Ab/Eb   Eb   F

We'll get close to some-day.

(Repeat chorus two times)

—*Contributed by Max and Marcia Nass*

Lesson 1

LOVE LESSON 1

Imagining a Loving World

Say, "Today we are starting a new values unit. The value we will be exploring is Love." Ask:

- Who thinks love is important? Why?
- Would it be a different world if everyone were loving toward everyone else?

Imagining a Loving World

Lead the students in this imagining exercise. Say the following, pausing at the dots. "Today I would like you to think about someone who is loving and kind. It can be a real person in your life now, or a person who helped you before, or it can be a person that you have seen in the movies. Think about that person's attitude. . . . Picture that person helping. . . . Now I want you to imagine that everyone in the world was that loving and kind. . . . What would the world be like? . . . Now step into your imaginary plane of the mind, and fly through the blue sky. . . . Picture leaders of different nations and how they treat each other. . . . How would they be with the citizens of their countries? . . . Picture friends playing. . . . See the students on a playground and in the neighborhood. . . . Fly the plane over your own neighborhood . . . and now over this school. . . . Imagine what would be happening. . . . Now the plane circles and lands, and you are relaxed and in your place here again."

Discuss/Share

Give the students time to share what they pictured and experienced. With a class of younger students, the teacher might want to lead this activity. With older students, the teacher can instruct small groups to share and report back to the larger class.

Ask:

- In a loving world, what would everyone want for his or her family?
- In a loving world, what would the rulers/leaders want for the citizens?
- If all the leaders of countries were like this, would they start wars?
- In a loving world, would anybody be interested in war? Why or why not?

Activity

If time permits, instruct the students to draw a symbol or picture of a loving world or to make up a poem.

Love

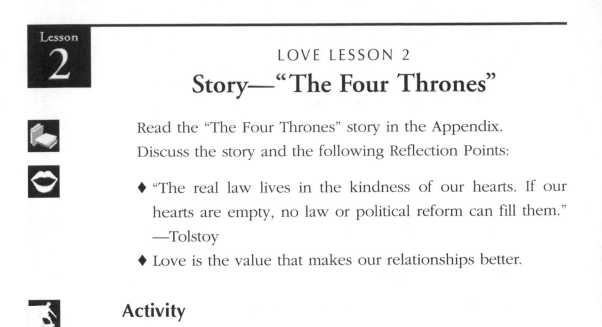

LOVE LESSON 2
Story—"The Four Thrones"

Read the "The Four Thrones" story in the Appendix.
Discuss the story and the following Reflection Points:

♦ "The real law lives in the kindness of our hearts. If our hearts are empty, no law or political reform can fill them." —Tolstoy

♦ Love is the value that makes our relationships better.

Activity

Ask the students to act out the story, draw it or write a personal journal page in response to the story.

LOVE LESSON 3
Mind Map a Loving World

Do the Imagining the Loving World exercise again.

Activity

Instruct the students to make a Mind Map of a loving world.

Love

LOVE LESSON 4

Mind Map a Non-Loving World

Discuss the following Reflection Point: "Our task must be to free ourselves . . . by widening our circle of compassion to embrace all living beings and all of nature."—Albert Einstein. Ask:

- What do you think Mr. Einstein meant?
- What happens when the circle of compassion is very small or does not exist?

Activity

Instruct the students to make a Mind Map of a non-loving world.

End the lesson with the following Relaxation/Focusing exercise. You may wish to say, "Many people live in places in the world that are non-loving. Would you like to do a relaxation exercise in which we send love to them?"

Sending Love Relaxation/Focusing Exercise

"Be Peace Stars for a few minutes and send love to people all over the world. . . . Think of the stars and imagine yourself to be just like them. . . . They are so beautiful in the sky, and they sparkle and shine . . . quietly and peacefully. . . . Relax your toes and legs. . . . Relax your stomach . . . and your shoulders. . . . Relax your arms . . . and your face. . . . We are safe; a soft light of peace surrounds you. . . . Inside you are like a beautiful little star. . . . You,

Love

the tiny star inside, are full of peaceful light . . . full of love. . . . We can all send love and peace any time we want. . . . Let yourself be full of loving energy. . . . Send that love to people all over the world. . . . Let the body relax. . . . Take in more love. . . . You are focused. . . . You are contributing to a better world. . . . Let your mind be still. . . . And then see yourself sitting here again."

Lesson 5

LOVE LESSON 5

Story

The teacher can select stories to read about people's love serving as inspiration to do something special—for another person, for someone who is ill or for an animal. There are many books. Pick one popular in your culture or one easily accessible.

After reading the story, discuss it with the students. Point out how the person's love motivated him or her to act in a courageous or kind way.

For example, in Zimbabwe, Natalie Ncube's class of high-school boys read Valentin Katayev's short story, "Rainbow Flower." This story is about a girl who became lost and met an old woman. The old woman gave her a magic Rainbow Flower that could make any wish come true. The flower had seven petals, each allowing a wish. The girl wasted six of them and used the seventh, the last one, to cure a crippled boy.

Mrs. Ncube noted: "After the story had been read in class, the development of the girl's character was discussed. The pupils noticed that with the first six petals the girl's character deteriorated because of jealousy, envy and unnecessary pride. Only

when she was left with one petal did she become more thoughtful and try to use the petal 'wisely.' While she was wishing for
material things, she felt unhappy, dissatisfied and unfulfilled.
When she saw the lame boy, many values emerged."

Follow-up Activities:

Class Debate. Do selfish desires bring satisfaction and happiness in life?

Draw a table of the negativities and virtues of the girl (or the
central character in a story selected by the teacher).

Homework. Write a story, "What I Would Do if I Had the
Rainbow Flower."

Draw the Rainbow Flower and write your words on the petals.

LOVE LESSON 6

Words of the Heart

Lesson
6

Say, "The value that we will continue to explore today is Love.
Let's start by playing with some of the combined words having
to do with the heart." Ask:

- Have you heard of hard-hearted, softhearted, bighearted?
  What does each mean?
- Can you think of any more? . . . Great!
  (If not mentioned, you may want to add small-hearted,
  mean-hearted, halfhearted.)

Eight-Year-Old Activity: Instruct students to make a "heart person" from pipe cleaners and to tell their parents what the heart
person would say. If there is time, they can draw a couple of

Love

heart people and write down what each one would say.

Nine to Eleven Activity: Instruct students to make a small story-book with the characters as hearts of different kinds. They can illustrate the different hearted characters on each page and write a statement about what that heart would say. You may want the students to share one page of their completed book in front of the class or group.

Twelve to Fourteen Language Arts Activity: Continue the above discussion by asking students to think of characters in literary works they have been studying recently. What actions of the characters reveal they are mean-hearted, bighearted, etc.? Ask which of those characters they would like to join them in their world now, and why. If time allows, they could write a short essay on this topic.

Lesson 7

LOVE LESSON 7

Love Is Caring, Love Is Kindness

Discuss the following Reflection Point: Love is caring, love is sharing. Then, ask the students for their ideas on little things people can do that are kind. Select something to do. The students may want to log on to the Living Values Education Program Website to share their kind acts or projects that contribute to a better world.

Activity

Do little things that are kind—make cards for your caregivers on special days, make cards for a child who has moved, share

Love

a dessert, help someone. Several students who are friends could befriend a new child in their class, showing the child around, introducing him or her and playing with him or her at break. The class may wish to select a Secret Friend for the remainder of the week.

Secret Friend Activity: Each student can write his or her name on a small scrap of paper and put it in a box. Allow each student to choose one name from the box, being careful not to select his or her own name. During the week, each student is to note down positive behaviors and qualities about the student whose name they have chosen.

At the end of the week, each student can make a card (younger students may wish to make a picture of the other student) and write down some of his or her positive notes. If a respectful atmosphere already exists within the class, allow each student to share what is written. The students in the class can guess for whom it is written.

—Contributed by Pilar Quera Colomina and Sabine Levy

LOVE LESSON 8
Conflict Resolution

Lesson
8

Begin the lesson with a song on Love.

Then refer to the content of Peace Lesson 16 by putting up the poster or drawing on the board the diagram used during the lesson on feeling valued, hurt or angry. Ask:

- Do you remember this diagram? Who can tell me about it?

Love

- Can you think of some examples when you've seen this happen?

Discuss the following Reflection Points in relationship to the diagram:

♦ When I am full of love, anger runs away.
♦ When my words give flowers instead of thorns, I create a better world.
♦ When we feel strong inside, it's easy to be loving.

Activity

Assign small groups of students to create a short skit about a conflict relevant at school or in the neighborhood. Ask them to introduce a "freeze-and-replay" element into the skit—in which the actors return to the actions and words in the play when the conflict started and when a loving attitude would have affected the outcome. They are then to inject that loving attitude into the replay.

NOTE TO TEACHER

If the students enjoy doing this, the technique can be used when something is going amiss on the playground or in the playroom. The teacher can say: "Freeze—let's have a replay. What was the starting point?" This is an interesting element to include when doing conflict resolution.

LOVE LESSON 9

Love Is Understanding

Discuss the following Reflection Point: Love means I can be kind, caring and understanding. Note to the students that in an earlier lesson, they practiced listening. Today you want them to think of a time someone really listened to them. Ask:

- How did they show they were listening?
- What was their attitude?
- What did that feel like?

Activity

Ask the students to form pairs with someone they do not know very well. One student is to share something he or she enjoyed doing when younger, or something that interested the student. The other student is to listen. They then exchange roles. Each person can share what he or she discovered about the other person to the class or a small group.

Homework: Listen to someone in your family and stay full of love as you listen. Listen to an adult one day and to a sister or brother another day.

—*Contributed by Marcia Maria Lins de Medeiros*

Love

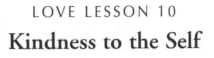

LOVE LESSON 10
Kindness to the Self

Discuss

- What do you love in yourself?
- How can people be loving or kind to themselves?

Eight to Eleven Activity: Do one of the things you discussed above.

Twelve to Fourteen Activity: Write a short letter to yourself, saying what you appreciate about yourself and giving yourself your best advice.

—*Based on a contribution by Marcia Maria Lins de Medeiros*

LOVE LESSON 11
I Am Lovable and Capable

Say, "I want you to think about this Reflection Point: Everyone in this room is lovable and capable." Ask:

- How do you feel when you feel lovable and capable at the same time?
- How would you feel inside if you felt that this was true for you all the time?
- What would you not worry about?
- Everyone in this room is naturally lovable and capable.
- What would our behavior be like if we all remembered this all the time?

Love

- What kinds of things would we do?
- What kinds of things would we not do?
- When do you feel lovable?
- When do you feel capable?
- What kinds of things can you do that create those feelings?
- What kinds of things can you say to yourself to help you feel this way?

Activity

Paint an abstract picture of lovable and capable feelings, or write a short essay or poem entitled "I Am Lovable and Capable."

LOVE LESSON 12

Kinds of Love

Lesson

12

Discuss/Share

- What do you have love for? (love for the self, friends, family, girl/boyfriends, nature, animals, possessions, playing, sports, humanity, your own country, the world, peace, etc.).
- What is love?
- Let's see if we can name some different kinds of love. (Self-love, brotherly love, platonic love, romantic love, love for the family, universal love, love for nature, love for humanity, etc.)

Discuss the following Reflection Point: I can have love for myself, love for my family, love for others, love for my country, love for my goals and love for the world—all at the same time. Ask: "Is that possible?"

Love

Eight to Ten Activity: The teacher can relate one of the kinds of love above to an aspect the students are studying—perhaps a story, poem or social studies unit.

Eleven to Twelve Activity: Take up the aspect of "love for goals." Ask the students what their goals are—in school currently or perhaps for their family, or ask what goals they hope to achieve when they are older. Ask them what they can do now that will affect obtaining those goals in the future. Ask them to write down two things they can do this week toward achieving those goals.

Thirteen to Fourteen Activity: Relate "romantic love" and "platonic love" to works recently studied in literature, or refer to classics, or literature or oral stories from the culture of the students.

NOTE TO TEACHER

Do the above activity if the following activity is not appropriate for students of this age in your particular culture.

If the teacher is comfortable doing this, ask the students what they think the rules of platonic love should be now. What do they think the rules of romantic love should be? What should people never do? (This is an opportunity to confirm that any violence toward a boyfriend or girlfriend is wrong.) How old do they think people should be when they get married? (Students usually say an age which is older than one would expect!) What are the advantages of waiting to get married? (Students have more time for school; with a better education, they can provide more for their families, etc.)

LOVE LESSON 13

A Trustworthy Friend

Discuss the following Reflection Point: Love is being a trustworthy friend. Then ask:

- What does that mean?
- What do we want in a friend?
- What makes a friend trustworthy?
- What does someone do that makes us think we cannot trust that person?
- How do you show that you are a trustworthy friend?

Bring up another Reflection Point: Love for others means I want what is good for them.

- What does that mean?
- How do you show your friends you want what is good for them?

Some teachers may want to link the above two Reflection Points. That will depend on your students and whether you feel they need to hear the following. Concept: Some students have a common misperception that part of being trustworthy is to hide information from adults when a friend is in serious trouble. Friends who are trustworthy also want what is good for their friend. That means if a friend is in serious trouble, one should take action to help. An example of this is telling the teacher or a parent that someone is thinking of hurting himself or herself. Ask, "Can you think of any other examples when a friend should

Love

take action to help?" Hurting someone else would be another important answer. If the students are age eleven and older, another appropriate example is: Friends don't let their friends drink and drive. Point: When we love someone, we want that person to be safe.

Lesson 14

LOVE LESSON 14
Artistic Expression

Choose a form of artistic expression to express your thoughts on this value.

Activity One: Create a slogan on the value of Love. Groups of three students can work together to make banners. Hang them on the walls.

Activity Two: Create a dance on universal love.

Activity Three: Create a song.

Lesson 15

LOVE LESSON 15
Creating a Story

Activity

Ask the students to write a story entitled "A Day in the Life of a Child in a World Full of Love." What is the child's morning like at home, his or her day at school, while with friends? What do people say to this child during the day?

After the stories are written, students can read them aloud for a couple days. As they read, other students can record what people said to each other in their loving worlds. Create a list to post on the wall. The teacher may want to add a few. Give students six dots or permission to make six marks by the remarks they would most like to hear. Make a new list of the most popular remarks and post it on the wall for awhile. Ask: "Could we say any of these statements in school? Could we say these at home?

LOVE LESSON 16

A Mural

Lesson

16

Activity

Tell the students they can make a quick mural as a group. Divide the class into teams of students. One team can be responsible for the sky, another for the ground and trees, another for buildings, another for animals and another for people. Do the Imagining a Loving World exercise again, inserting a little more dialogue on the beauty of the sky, meadows, trees, buildings and animals. Tell them to pretend they are in that world while they are painting.

—Contributed by Diana Hsu

Love

Lesson 17

LOVE LESSON 17

Optional Project

The class may wish to do a project of its own. Ask the students what they wish to do. What are the needs in the community? Would they want to rotate being tutors to younger students for twenty minutes a day?

FOUR

Tolerance

4. TOLERANCE UNIT

Tolerance

Tolerance Reflection Points

♦ Peace is the goal, tolerance is the method.

♦ Tolerance is being open and receptive to the beauty of differences.

♦ Tolerance is mutual respect through mutual understanding.

♦ The seeds of intolerance are fear and ignorance.

♦ The seed of tolerance, love, is watered by compassion and care.

♦ Those who know how to appreciate the good in people and situations have tolerance.

♦ Tolerance recognizes individuality and diversity while removing divisive masks and defusing tension created by ignorance. (For twelve- to fourteen-year-old students only.)

♦ Tolerance is the ability to face difficult situations.

♦ To tolerate life's inconveniences is to let go, be light, make others light and move on.

Tolerance Unit

GOAL: To increase tolerance through understanding others.
OBJECTIVES:

❑ To understand that each one of us is different, and to do the "walk in your moccasins" exercise with another student.

❑ To discuss feelings that arise when a person is discriminated against.

❑ To interview and listen to others.

GOAL: To increase knowledge and appreciation of different cultures.

OBJECTIVES:

❏ To understand that every culture and race is valuable, as is every ray of the rainbow.

❏ To participate in discussions about the Tolerance Reflection Points and be able to talk about two or more of them.

❏ To learn about two or more cultures other than their own, through hearing stories, learning songs and participating in some form of artistic expression of that culture.

GOAL: To develop socially conscious skills for increased social cohesion.

OBJECTIVES:

❏ To understand that the seeds of intolerance are fear and ignorance.

❏ To write and discuss their advice about how people should treat other people.

❏ To become more aware of acts of tolerance and intolerance by collecting current news stories; to make a class collage of acts of tolerance and to locate on a map acts of intolerance.

❏ To become more aware of intolerant attitudes, if they exist on the playground, and work toward a positive resolution of the problems.

❏ To be able to generate at least one "benevolently assertive response" to a disciminatory statement during a class exercise.

❏ To become aware of another meaning of tolerance, meaning to tolerate difficulties, and discuss "self-talk" that is helpful.

Tolerance

Tolerance Lessons

Continue to play a song daily. Sing or listen to a song that speaks of the world's peoples as family. For example, "One Family" by Red Grammer speaks of the human world family as "sisters and brothers, a coat of many colors."

Do one of the Relaxation/Focusing exercises every day or every several days, as suitable for your class. The students may enjoy making up their own.

Lesson
1

TOLERANCE LESSON 1
A Lack of Tolerance

Explain: "In the next few weeks (or whatever length of time), we will be learning about tolerance. In the dictionary, tolerance is defined as 'a fair and objective attitude toward those whose opinions, practices, race, religion, nationality, or the like, differ from one's own; freedom from bigotry.'" *(Random House College Dictionary)*

"Do you remember the World Cake you made when we were studying peace? Many of the cakes had the ingredients of peace, respect and love. Real tolerance is based on those ingredients."

State the following Reflection Points:

♦ Tolerance is mutual respect through mutual understanding.
♦ Tolerance has been called an essential factor for world peace. Peace is the goal, tolerance is the method.

Tolerance

The teacher may wish to share a little or all of the background information below, depending on the ages of the students.

Background: The year 1995 was designated The Year of Tolerance by the United Nations on the grounds that tolerance is an "essential factor for world peace." The United Nations General Assembly made this decision . . . "in light of the resurgence of: ethno-nationalist conflict; discrimination against minority groups; acts of xenophobia, particularly against refugees and asylum-seekers, migrant workers, and immigrant racist organizations and ideologies; and acts of racial violence . . . intolerance expressed through marginalization and exclusion from society of vulnerable groups, or violence and discrimination against them. . . . Intolerance . . . is the rejection of differences among individuals and cultures. When intolerance becomes collective or institution-alized, it erodes democratic principles and poses a threat to world peace . . . It is essential to recall that the basic human values that unite us are stronger than the forces that pull us apart."

Eight to Eleven Story: "I'm going to read you a story about some imaginary people who did not have tolerance." Read "The Shorties and the Tallies" in the Appendix.

Twelve to Fourteen Subject Content: Select one of your favorite stories, or select a story or work from the curriculum on intolerance. You may wish to choose a piece by one of your country's authors. If you decide to read "The Shorties and the Tallies," ask students to identify the elements that cause strife and discrimination. Ask if they see parallels to a real situation that the class has studied.

Discuss the story or literary work in relation to the following Reflection Points:

Tolerance

♦ Tolerance is mutual respect through mutual understanding.

♦ The seeds of intolerance are fear and ignorance.

Ask: "What would the world be like if everyone had tolerance?" Acknowledge their answers, and end with a song.

Lesson 2

TOLERANCE LESSON 2

Real Stories

Stories: Read to the students or they can read a story about real people who experienced intolerance. For younger students, one such story is "Molly's Pilgrim" by Barbara Cohen. Older students (thirteen- and fourteen-year-olds) could read parts of Nelson Mandela's "Walk to Freedom" or another work from your language arts Tolerance lesson curriculum.

Activity

Talk with students about their feelings regarding the story they have read.

Ask them to write a few lines and illustrate their thoughts or write a short personal essay.

End with a song on tolerance.

TOLERANCE LESSON 3
Walking in Your Shoes

Activity

Ask members of the class to pair up with someone they do not normally play or work with and to decide who is going to be A and B. This is a silent exercise to discover what it is like to pretend to be somebody else.

Explain that the A's are going to go for a walk for ten minutes (the A's keep time). The B's are going to follow them and copy everything they do—from the length, speed and rhythm of their stride and the way they place their feet to the way they hold their hands and swing their arms. They will look and listen to whatever the A's look at and listen to. In other words, B is going to spend ten minutes discovering what it is like to be A.

After ten minutes they can stop and talk, and B can tell A what he or she discovered—what changed when pretending to be A.

Then reverse roles and repeat the above. When they get back, ask for discoveries and put them up on the board.

—Contributed by Diana Beaver

TOLERANCE LESSONS 4 TO 9
A Rainbow

Concept: Compare the variety of races, cultures and individuals to a rainbow. The rainbow would not be nearly as beautiful if it were missing one or two colors—in fact, it would not be a rainbow with only one color. The human family is like a rainbow; it comes with a wonderful variety of colors. Each culture and tradition has something important to contribute.

Discuss one of the following Reflection Points each day prior to doing the following activities:

♦ Peace is the goal, tolerance is the method.
♦ Tolerance is being open and receptive to the beauty of differences.
♦ The seed of tolerance, love, is watered by compassion and care.
♦ Those who know how to appreciate the good in people and situations have tolerance.
♦ Tolerance recognizes individuality and diversity while removing divisive masks and defusing tension created by ignorance. (For twelve- to fourteen-year-old students only.)

Activity

Ask students to make a rainbow. They can make a large one of paper to be placed on the wall, or they can make individual ones.

Activity

Do several lessons on informative stories about the various cultures in your area or country, selecting fiction or nonfiction stories appropriate to the ages of the students. Discuss the information afterward. Put the culture of each story you read in a different ray of the rainbow. Ask:

- What values are important to this culture?
- How do they show that?

Activity

Ask the students to make up a poem or a song about the human world family as a rainbow.

Activity

Make figures in traditional dress of the cultures you are studying. Place them around the rainbow. Older students could make symbols from that culture, describe relevant characteristics or write down significant events in the history of that culture.

Activity

Perhaps for one week, one person from a different culture could come in and talk with the class. He or she might be willing to bring in a traditional treat or share a song, poem or piece of art from that culture. Perhaps one or two of the guests can teach you a dance.

Homework: During these lessons begin to watch the news and find pictures and articles in the newspaper about examples of intolerance and tolerance.

Tolerance

TOLERANCE LESSON 10
A Collage of Tolerance, A Map of Intolerance

Activity

Ask the students to continue to watch the news and find pictures and articles in the newspaper about examples of intolerance and tolerance. Ask them to observe situations of tolerance and intolerance around them. During the time they report their findings, issues for discussion will come up. This will be an opportunity for the class to generate ways to deal with the situation(s) in a manner that promotes harmony.

A collage on tolerance and a map on intolerance can be developed as students continue to bring in information. Their drawings, poems and pictures can be added to a collage on the wall during the weeks they are studying tolerance. Place pins or dots on a map for instances of intolerance.

—*Contributed by Pilar Quera Colomina and Sabine Levy*

NOTE TO TEACHER

The teacher is responsible for providing a tolerant atmosphere in which the students can thrive. Be attentive to all forms of exclusion, selfishness and meanness that mask fear and ignorance. Establish the spirit of tolerance through dialogue and understanding.

Help students put an end to intolerance by encouraging them to appreciate the beauty of diversity and the richness it brings.

Emphasize that listening to others is the first step toward tolerance. Help them listen, be tolerant, and have the aim of understanding and achieving a positive and accurate solution. Continue to reinforce respect while helping them understand others.

When conflicts arise that have a hint of intolerance, discuss them.

- What are little things that people do that indicate prejudice or intolerance? (You can't play. It's my ball. She's not good enough to . . . etc.)

- What can we do to change that?

Make the point that tolerance is the ability to face situations and offer creative solutions.

—Contributed by Pilar Quera Colomina and Sabine Levy

TOLERANCE LESSON 11

Discrimination

Lesson 11

Awareness Activity—Sharing. Ask students about the lack of tolerance of differences they have noticed at school or in society. Ask students if they can think of an example of intolerance. If they cannot, mention, in age-appropriate terms, one that they might be aware of.

- Are some people tolerated less than others?
- Are some discriminated against? On what basis?
- Have you ever been discriminated against?
- How did it feel?

Tolerance

- What attitude would you like everyone to have toward each other?
- If someone is really popular, will people be more likely to tolerate that person?
- What kinds of things can we say to ourselves so we can have more tolerance of others?

Eight to Nine Activity: Write a few sentences about how people feel when they have been discriminated against, and draw a picture. Then write two sentences of advice about how people should act.

Ten to Fourteen Activity: Write a short personal essay about feeling discriminated against or being treated unfairly. Ask each student to think of his or her advice about how people should treat each other. The teacher may wish to instruct students to focus their advice, that is, if the students are studying the structure of the government, what would their advice be to the leaders of the country? Or what would their advice be to other students of the world, parents, teachers or adults? The students could read their advice in small groups, and each group could then make a slogan. Draw the slogans on posters or long pieces of paper and place them on the walls.

Lesson 12

TOLERANCE LESSON 12

Walking in Your Shoes

During history, social studies or literature, ask students to identify a character who is different from them. To develop

Tolerance

understanding, ask them to write a short story as if they were that person, explaining the beliefs and reasons behind that character's actions.

Pen Pals

Having pen pals is a wonderful method for students to truly understand that other people around the world are much the same as they are.

TOLERANCE LESSON 13
Understanding

Activity

Pair up students with someone with whom they do not usually work. Tell them to interview each other. Then let two pairs form a group. Each student should take a turn pretending to be his or her partner, telling about "himself" or "herself" and answering questions.

TOLERANCE LESSON 14
Disarming Prejudice

Discuss/Share

Ask the students if they have heard mean or prejudiced things said in the past. If the answer is "yes," ask them if they would like to think about ways to change that in the future. Then ask:

- What prejudiced or mean things have you heard people say at school? (List those quickly on the board.)
- What usually happens when that type of thing is said?

Summarize: Say, "So, sometimes when someone says something aggressive, feelings are hurt, and things get even worse. Sometimes when one is aggressive, the other person says or does something aggressive back."

If they talk about the insulted party going away and saying nothing, say, "Sometimes when someone says something aggressive, the other person goes away. The other's response appears passive." Ask:

- But how does he or she feel inside? (Acknowledge their responses.)

Explain: Say, "When someone says something mean, there are generally three types of responses. You have described aggressive responses and passive responses. The other type of response is called an assertive response.

"You have been learning about assertive responses already. When someone does something mean and you say, 'I don't want you to do that; I want you to stop,' that is an assertive response. You are being assertive during conflict resolution when you say to someone, with respect, 'I don't like it when you _____, and I want you to _____.' You are also being assertive when you use the 'I feel' response we practiced in the unit on Respect: 'I feel _____ when you _____ because _____.'" Ask:

Tolerance

- Can anyone take an example given and see if you can think of something to say using that last sentence, the "I feel" sentence?

Give the students time to do the above. Positively remark on their efforts and help them as needed.

Say, "Very often we only want to share our feelings with people who are friends or people we know very well. So sometimes you will be uncomfortable using the 'I feel' statement and will choose not to use it. However, sometimes people say mean things, and we just want to say something back." Ask:

- What happens if we say something back which is aggressive? (Acknowledge their responses: people become even angrier; there is more resentment; more fights; retaliation begins.)
- What happens when we are passive? (Some may say: People have no respect for you and treat you worse; you feel like you have no courage.)

Say, "I want you to put on your thinking caps and think of assertive responses that could be said to these mean, prejudiced remarks we have listed on the board. But I want you not only to think of something that is not aggressive, and something that is not passive, I want you also to think of something benevolently assertive!"

Then, ask students to generate remarks that could be said in response; remarks that offer a more tolerant view that could be considered assertive yet benevolent; not aggressive, but not wishy-washy either. Examples are, "It wouldn't be such a nice

Tolerance

world if we were all clones," or "What would you do if you were in her place?" Ask for a couple volunteers to model the responses. Encourage them to stay in self-respect as they repeat their remarks. Lead the applause. Ask students to make a list of the best supportive comebacks. Role-play a couple of scenes using the responses generated.

Discuss the following Reflection Point: The seed of tolerance, love, is watered by compassion and care.

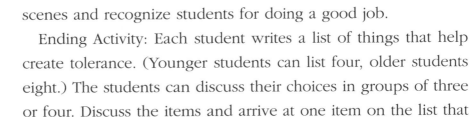

TOLERANCE LESSON 15
The Key

Discuss the Reflection Point: Those who know how to appreciate the good in people and situations have tolerance.

Follow-up Activity: Generate and practice supportive comebacks for ten minutes or more, practicing the skill learned in the last lesson. The teacher or students can say comments they heard on the playground. Others can offer replies which are assertive and full of self-respect. Practicing these until they are comfortable makes them more likely to be used. Role-play a couple of scenes and recognize students for doing a good job.

Ending Activity: Each student writes a list of things that help create tolerance. (Younger students can list four, older students eight.) The students can discuss their choices in groups of three or four. Discuss the items and arrive at one item on the list that is most important for tolerance.

TOLERANCE LESSON 16

Tolerating Difficulties

Explain: Another definition of the word tolerance is "the act or capacity of enduring; endurance: My tolerance for noise is limited." (*Random House College Dictionary.*)

The Reflection Points for this kind of tolerance are:

♦ Tolerance is the ability to face difficult situations.

♦ To tolerate life's inconveniences is to let go, be light, make others light and move on.

In this form, tolerance is facing difficult situations by seeing them from a different perspective: as molehills, not mountains. Adopting that perspective, of course, would depend on the nature of the situation. Express to the students that sometimes what appears as a formidable challenge—"a mountain"—may, in retrospect, have only been "a molehill." It's a matter of seeing the circumstance in the overall scheme of things.

Discuss/Share

Ask the students to share "self-talk" or methods that help them face or accommodate difficulties. Positively reinforce their sharing.

Activity

Select a biography of someone who has demonstrated exceptional tolerance in her or his life. Read aloud passages that illustrate the value of tolerance. Or the students could write a short story or personal essay on something they have tolerated.

Tolerance

TOLERANCE LESSON 17

A Pretend Immigration

Activity

Ask the students to make up a story about immigrating to a pretend country. Ask them to talk about how they want to be treated and how they want their parents to be treated. Younger students may wish to illustrate their story with a drawing. Older students can make images of tolerance and add them to the collage.

—*Contributed by Marcia Maria Lins de Medeiros*

OPTIONAL TOLERANCE LESSON 18

A Cultural Celebration

Plan a celebration of different cultures, with songs, dances and food from a variety of cultures. It may be more convenient to have assembly. In class, ask the students to stand in a circle and share just a couple of sentences about what they discovered and really appreciate about a culture different than their own.

FIVE

Happiness

5. HAPPINESS UNIT

Happiness

Happiness Reflection Points

♦ When I have love and peace inside, happiness just comes.

♦ Happiness is a state of peace in which there is no upheaval or violence.

♦ Give happiness and take happiness.

♦ When there is a feeling of hope, there is happiness.

♦ Good wishes for everyone gives happiness inside.

♦ Happiness naturally comes with pure and selfless actions.

♦ Lasting happiness is a state of contentment within.

♦ When one is content with oneself, happiness comes automatically.

♦ When my words express "give flowers instead of thorns," I create a happier world.

♦ Happiness follows giving happiness, sorrow follows giving sorrow.

Happiness Unit

GOAL: To enjoy the experience of happiness.

OBJECTIVES:

❏ To enjoy the music of happy songs.

❏ To enjoy playing a couple of games.

❏ To participate in an exercise of imagining a world of happiness.

❏ To paint or dance the feeling of happiness.

GOAL: To increase knowledge about happiness.
OBJECTIVES:

- ❏ To participate in discussions about Happiness Reflection Points and be able to talk about two or more of them.
- ❏ To reflect about when they are happy and to write about their feelings.
- ❏ To think about words that create happiness and words that cause harm.
- ❏ To think about actions that contribute to the happiness of the self, others and the world.
- ❏ To reflect on lasting happiness versus happiness from material objects.
- ❏ To reflect on the relationship between happiness and trying to do our best.
- ❏ To reflect on their own self-talk and how to encourage themselves more.

GOAL: To explore skills for giving happiness.
OBJECTIVES:

- ❏ To do at least three actions at school that give happiness to others.
- ❏ To make up a story on giving happiness as part of a group.
- ❏ To do at least four actions at home that give happiness to members of their family.
- ❏ To think about the effects of excluding versus including others.
- ❏ To generate their own secret for giving happiness.

Happiness

Happiness Lessons

Continue to play a song daily.

Do one of the Relaxation/Focusing exercises every day or every several days, as suitable for your class. The students may enjoy making up their own.

Lesson

1

HAPPINESS LESSON 1

Happiness

Play a happy song as the students enter, and explain: "In the next four weeks (or whatever length of time), we're going to explore the value of Happiness.

As the teacher, first share something that makes you happy. Then ask: "What makes you happy?"

List the students' ideas on the board. Help them identify differences in feelings—for example, feelings that are exciting versus feelings that are deeper and more long-term.

Eight to Ten Activity: Make a zigzag happy book, or write sentences, "I feel happy when . . ."

—*Contributed by Linda Heppenstall*

Eleven to Fourteen Activity: Contrast Poetry. Ask students to brainstorm vocabulary associated with happiness and sadness. They can use a dictionary and thesaurus to find synonyms and antonyms. As a group or as individuals, students can write poetry to take the reader from one feeling or idea to its opposite.

—*Contributed by Ruth Liddle*

HAPPINESS LESSON 2

What Makes Happiness?

Play a happy song. Ask the students to join you in singing. Discuss the following Reflection Points:

◆ When I have love and peace inside, happiness just comes.

◆ When one is content with oneself, happiness comes automatically.

◆ Happiness is a state of peace in which there is no upheaval or violence.

Ask:

• Can we create our own happiness? How?

• When do you feel most content?

• What kinds of things do you think to increase the feeling of happiness?

• What kinds of things can you do alone that make you feel happy?

Activity

Play happy music and ask the students to paint the feeling of being happy.

Activity Option for Older Students: Ask the students to form small groups and discuss a topic of interest that arose during the discussion.

Happiness

HAPPINESS LESSON 3
Words and Unicorns

Discuss

- What do your friends say that makes you happy?
- What do you like to hear?

Think about the following Reflection Point: When my words "give flowers instead of thorns," I create a happier world. Then, ask:

- What kinds of words are like thorns?
- Can words hurt people or cause harm? (Yes.)

There is a child's poem: "Sticks and stones will break my bones, but words will never hurt me." An adult changed this to: "Sticks and stones will break my bones, but words hurt forever inside." Ask:

- How do you feel when you hear someone hurt someone else's feelings?
- What kinds of words would you like to hear around you?
- What do you say that gives happiness to others?

Unicorns

Tell the following story: "Today I have a short tale about unicorns. It is a participatory story, because I want you to use your imagination. . . . One day, thirty (use the number of students in the classroom at the time) unicorns come to our school. We go outside, and a unicorn comes up to each one of us. You can imagine our surprise to see unicorns, and so many! These unicorns are silvery white and have large wings. They look very strong. Each unicorn holds out one wing so we can each have help climbing onto its back. Once each one of us is safely seated on the unicorn's back, it starts to fly. Up we go! They fly to the place where they live—they must know that we've been studying these values and there was one on happiness today. The unicorns decided to take us to a Land of Happiness. Well, when they start to land, we can see how beautiful it is . . . and there are all these students there your age! They come to welcome you! They are playing great music. And you join them in a picnic. . . . Delicious food! . . . And then you play games. . . . There are different kinds of games, so each one of you can join the one that you like to play. . . . Afterward you sit on the grass and talk. One of students of this land tells you that in their world, they look at everyone like a beautiful flower. They see each one as more beautiful than the next. . . . As you sit there, you experience that everyone has love for you and for every other person there. . . . Then one of the students leans a little closer to you and whispers, 'I'm going to tell you another secret about happiness'. . . . And then he or she tells you a secret of happiness. . . . Only you hear this particular secret of happiness. . . . What was whispered? . . . The unicorns tell us that it's time to go, and they extend their wings again. The students wave good-bye to us as we fly off, and we wave good-bye to them. And, before you know it, we're back at school again and sitting in these chairs."

Happiness

Discuss/Share

Allow a few minutes for students to share their thoughts and images. Tell the students that the child who whispered to you said: The secret to being happy is "Give happiness and take happiness, don't give sorrow and take sorrow." Ask:

- "What does that mean?"

Activity

Write a story on "The Secrets of Happiness." Perhaps draw or paint a picture to accompany the story.

Lesson 4

HAPPINESS LESSON 4

Games

Ask a few students to share their "secrets of happiness."

Activity

Play a game or do something that creates a mood of happiness. For instance, play a game that everyone loves, one that usually brings lots of laughter. Think of the games that you enjoyed as a child.

You may want to try an unusual version of musical chairs. Change the rules by allowing more than one person to sit in a chair. The students circle around the chairs when the music is playing, and then sit in the chairs when the music stops. Each time the music stops, another chair is removed. In this version, when the music stops and there are not enough chairs, instead of that child being out of the game, he or she simply sits on the lap of someone already seated on a chair. You may want to stop the game when there are four or five people seated on one chair! In many countries, you may need to play one round with girls, another with boys. There are many suitable games that are fun. Play one that you enjoy, too.

HAPPINESS LESSON 5

Happiness at Home

Lesson

5

Discuss/Share

- Can you remember a time when you helped someone and that made you happy?
- Did anyone ever surprise you in a way that made you happy?
- What do your parents say that makes you happy?
- What would your parents like to hear from you?
- How many of you have older brothers and sisters? What kinds of things did you like to do with them when you were little?
- Do you think your younger brothers and sisters would like to do that with you?
- How can we contribute to other people's happiness?

Say, "Let's list all the things people your age can do to give happiness at home." List their responses on the board as they

Happiness

call out answers. Group them in different categories, such as Words, Activities with Sisters and Brothers, and Actions.

Further questions for twelve- to fourteen-year-old students:

- What can you genuinely say to your parents that they would like to hear?
- If a person gave you several compliments, but you did not feel that person meant it, how would you feel?
- When a person gives you one compliment, but you feel that person really means it, how do you feel?
- Is it important to be genuine? Why?
- When you give a compliment and are genuine, how do you feel inside?

Activity

Play another game that the students enjoy.

Play a happy song.

Homework: Tell students their homework this week is to give happiness by doing three or four good deeds at home without telling anyone. As the week progresses, ask how their homework is going. (A lot of joy is created in the classroom with this activity.) The students may tell you that someone found out. Tell them that is okay, but do another secret good deed.

Lesson 6

HAPPINESS LESSON 6

Stories

Read aloud or ask students to read tales about happiness. Think of your favorite childhood stories about happiness. The

Happiness

teacher may want to select folktales or old legends about happiness. Discuss the story after reading it.

Eight to Eleven Story: Read "The Heart School" or "Finding the Magic." The former can be found in the Appendix; the latter is the published version of the story, developed further and rewritten by Barbara Ramsey.

Discuss/Share

In "The Heart School" story, Marc learns that it is important not to get upset with himself or anyone else. Ask:

- What did Marc learn to do? (To reflect briefly on what went wrong and then focus attention on progress and not mistakes.)
- Shall we do that, too?

Activity

Ask the students if they would like to make individual Happy Boxes or one Happy Box for the class. Make the boxes. Ask the students to write cards for the Happy Box, putting on each card a practical suggestion that would make them happier. Some classes may wish to make individual boxes and take them home. Other classes may wish to have one box for the entire class.

NOTE TO TEACHER

Many classes have discussion time during their "values time" at this point. You may wish to keep the Happy and Unhappy Boxes for your class if the students like them and appear to benefit from them. Either daily or weekly, take one card out of the Happy Box.

Happiness

Try this for at least four weeks. At least once a week, share your experiences and progress with each other, and also look for areas that need improvement. As the students discover new ways to be happy, ask them to write those down on new cards.

Lesson 7

HAPPINESS LESSON 7

Feelings

Discuss/Share

- What do we feel like doing when we are happy?
- What do we feel like doing when we are sad?
- How can we make ourselves feel better when we are sad?
- Is happiness a result of what we think or feel?
- Can we change the way we view things, or look at things another way?
- Where do feelings of happiness and sadness come from?
- How do you feel when you make others happy?

Ask about what the students are noticing from doing their Giving Happiness homework.

Activity Choice

Poem: Happiness is when _____.

Design a Happiness Badge.

Write an essay: Making Others Happy Brings Us Happiness, Too.

—Contributed by Linda Heppenstall

Happiness

HAPPINESS LESSON 8
Three Wishes

One of the classes at West Kidlington School discussed the Reflection Point, Lasting happiness is a state of contentment within. The students talked about how happiness is temporary when sought from outside sources, that is, from wealth, material possessions, status and relationships. They decided that lasting happiness is a state of contentment within that does not need to be fed by outside wants. Ask:

- What happens when our happiness depends on getting money from someone? Can that happiness be constant?
- What happens when our happiness depends on getting a new possession (game, dress, etc.)? Can our happiness be constant?
- How do you feel when you do not get something you want?
- How can you remain happy when you do not get something you want?
- How long does your happiness last when you get something new?
- What kinds of thoughts and actions create lasting happiness?

Activity

You have just liberated a genie from a bottle you found. The genie gives you the right to ask for three wishes: one for yourself, one for your family and one for the world. What are your three wishes? Create a drawing of your three wishes.

—Activity contributed by Marcia Maria Lins de Medeiros

Happiness

Lesson 9

HAPPINESS LESSON 9
Needs and Wants

Activity

Each student is to create a list of twelve things that give him or her happiness in life. As a class, discuss the difference between needs and wants. The students can discuss their choices in groups of three or four. Reduce the list to six items, then three items. Discuss it more to finally arrive at the one item on the list that gives the most happiness. The students can then write a letter of appreciation to the person connected with that item.

—Contributed by Ruth Liddle

Lesson 10

HAPPINESS LESSON 10
Happiness Is Sharing

Discuss the following Reflection Points:

♦ Happiness naturally comes with pure and selfless actions.
♦ Give happiness and take happiness.

Ask:

• What are pure and selfless actions?
• Can anyone think of examples? (This can be asked in relation to animals, the environment, family, friends and strangers.)

Ask the students to make something to give to someone. Examples are a friendly heart card for someone's birthday, a card for someone who is ill, a meal for the senior volunteers at your school, a poem for a friend, a happy heart card for a child you are tutoring in a younger class.

HAPPINESS LESSON 11
Talking to Myself

Build Concept: "Talking to Myself" is an acknowledgment of the process that occurs within every individual. We all talk to ourselves with a silent voice. This is called self-talk or inner dialogue. In this unit on Happiness, this is an important aspect to think about, as self-talk can be positive or negative, encouraging or discouraging.

Discuss/Share

"Today, let's think about the things we say to ourselves." Ask:

- What do you say when you make a mistake?
- What tone of voice do you use when you say that?
- What do you say to yourself when you're afraid that you'll miss the ball during a ball game or fail a test?
- If you make a mistake, do you feel better if you call yourself "Stupid," or if you say, "It's okay to make a mistake, all I have to do is correct it"?[2] There's no need to feel angry or sad—mistakes are simply things through which we learn.

---

[2]*This useful rule is from Thomas R. Bingham's Program for Affective Learning. ©1985.*

Happiness

- Does it help if you get angry?
- What happens to your feelings when you say, "I'll never be able to do it" or "I'll never make it"?
- Are the feelings different when you say, "This is a bit scary, but I'll do my best"?

Say, "Repeat the mistake rule with me, please: It's okay to make a mistake, all I have to do is correct it."

Make two columns on the board. Head one column with a sad face, the other with a happy face. Ask students to tell you what they say to themselves that makes them feel sad or unhappy; and what they say or could say to themselves to make them feel glad or happy. Ask:

- What can you say to create a happier feeling when working on an assignment?
- When walking alone?
- What differences do you notice in the tone of voice you use with yourself when you say things to make you happy?
- When working with others cooperatively?
- When trying to understand something disappointing?

Eight to Eleven Activity: Write a note to yourself, giving yourself advice about how you should talk to yourself.

Twelve to Fourteen Activity: Think about the Reflection Point: When there is a feeling of hope, there is happiness. Write a note to yourself, giving yourself advice about how you should talk to yourself. Consider situations when it is best to be encouraging, and tell yourself to persevere.

When working in a different subject area, the teacher might ask students about their inner dialogue. Continue to discuss this in a natural way, adding adaptive responses to the happy face list on the board.

HAPPINESS LESSON 12

Including and Excluding

Discuss/Share

- How do people feel when they are left out?
- Do you ever get left out?
- How do you feel?
- What do you do?
- What can you do when you see that someone has been left out?
- How can you be inclusive rather than exclusive?
- Are you happy when others are successful? (If not, ask why. Then, ask if they can think of another way to think about the situation—so they can be happy for the successful person. Perhaps bring up self-respect points. Or think, "She is getting the success she worked for; I will get the success I am working for.")

—Contributed by West Kidlington School

Discuss the following Reflection Points:

♦ Good wishes for everyone gives happiness inside.
♦ Happiness follows giving happiness, sorrow follows giving sorrow.

Happiness

Activity

As a group, make up two stories, one in which everyone gives sorrow and another in which everyone gives happiness. Start with the unhappy story first. Use the same beginning situation, and go around the room asking each student to add something to the story. Then make up a story in which everyone gives happiness. Have a good time!

Lesson 13

HAPPINESS LESSON 13

Quality

Concept: When you do your best, there is happiness. Quality thoughts lead to quality words. Quality words lead to quality actions.

Stimulus: Ask each student to choose a piece of work she or he is proud of. Or think about something which he or she does well.

Discuss

Talk about the importance of doing our best in work and at play.

Twelve to Fourteen Additional Discussion: Ask the students to discuss this in relation to the Reflection Point: When one is content with oneself, happiness comes automatically.

Activity

Form small groups of students. Ask each student to go around the circle saying something he or she appreciates about each student.

—*Contributed by Linda Heppenstall*

Happiness

HAPPINESS LESSON 14

A Giving Tree

Eight to Ten Activity: Make a Giving Tree. Instruct each student to make three certificates to hang on the tree, such as: Good for One Compliment, Certificate for Five Minutes Tutoring in Mathematics, Certificate for Pushing the Swing for Three Minutes, Good for One Game of Tether Ball, Good for Listening While You Practice Your Poem Three Times, Good for Showing the Latest Dance Step, etc. Each student could make up three certificates of something she or he has to offer. The certificates can be pinned to a paper tree posted on a bulletin board. The name of the person offering this service would be on the back of the certificate. Perhaps for three days in a row—when the students are finished with their work—they can silently select one certificate. Some of the students may want to create a giving tree at home: Good for One Hug, etc.

Eleven to Fourteen Activity: Ask students to make a Giving Tree. They may choose to make a small one for their younger sisters and brothers or one for the entire family. If so, they can ask other members of the family to participate. Or a group of students can decide to make a Giving Tree for a younger class of students. Or the class can decide to contribute to a special project in the area.

Happiness

HAPPINESS LESSON 15

More Secrets of Happiness

Discuss/Share

Introduce the saying: Happiness begins with me. Ask:

- What does this mean?

Repeat the Unicorn Story (from Happiness Lesson 3), but add a line at the close of the story. After the student whispers a secret of happiness, insert the line: "And then you share with your friend the secret of happiness you think is most important." Ask the students to illustrate or write their secrets of happiness: the one they were given and the one they shared.

HAPPINESS LESSON 16

Enact Happiness

Dance/Draw Happiness: Divide the students into two groups: those who want to create happiness through dance and those who want to create happiness through drawing or painting.

Optional Activity: Do a skit on happiness or play games.

End with a happy song.

SIX

Responsibility

6. RESPONSIBILITY UNIT

Responsibility

Responsibility Reflection Points

♦ If we want peace, we have the responsibility to be peaceful.

♦ If we want a clean world, we have the responsibility to care for nature.

♦ Responsibility is doing your share.

♦ Responsibility is accepting what is required and carrying out the task to the best of your ability.

♦ Responsibility is carrying out duties with integrity.

♦ When one is responsible, there is the contentment of having made a contribution.

♦ As a responsible person, I have something worthwhile to offer—so do others.

♦ A responsible person knows how to be fair, seeing that each gets a share.

♦ With rights there are responsibilities.

♦ Responsibility is not only something that obliges us, but also something that allows us to achieve what we wish.

♦ Each person can perceive his or her own world and look for the balance of rights and responsibilities.

♦ Global responsibility requires respect for all human beings.

♦ Responsibility is using our resources to generate a positive change.

Responsibility Unit

GOAL: To feel good about being responsible.
OBJECTIVES:

❏ To enjoy being responsible during a trust walk.

❏ To enjoy songs that link responsibility to caring.

❏ To enjoy participating in a play about responsibility.

GOAL: To increase knowledge about responsibility.
OBJECTIVES:

❏ To participate in discussions about the Responsibility Reflection Points and be able to talk about two or more of them.

❏ To make an "I Believe in . . ." booklet, exploring what they believe in, their rights and their responsibilities.

❏ To explore the concept of "walking my talk."

❏ To participate in a discussion about responsibility for the self.

❏ To make Mind Maps on the consequences of responsibility and irresponsibility.

❏ To discuss their contribution to their family, and to make a card or poem for a parent or write a personal journal page on showing responsibility.

❏ To discuss global responsibility.

GOAL: To develop skills for responsibility and participate responsibly in projects.
OBJECTIVES:

❏ To participate in a class responsibility project.

❏ To think about their goals as adults and to develop at least two immediate, small, practical actions in relation to that goal.

Responsibility

❏ To participate in a class discussion on how to encourage the self to be more responsible when one has not been.

❏ To make an image of what they believe in, and to carry through on one new action toward that goal.

Responsibility Lessons

Add to the list of Reflection Points using favorite sayings from your culture, from legends or quotes from respected individuals.

Continue to play a song daily. Play songs that touch on responsibility, perhaps ones from your cultural heritage. Older students respond well to "Circle of Life" by Elton John or "Conviction of the Heart" by Kenny Loggins.

Do one of the Relaxation/Focusing Exercises every day or every several days, as suitable for your class. The students may enjoy making up their own.

Lesson 1

RESPONSIBILITY LESSON 1

Trust Walk

Play a song as the students enter.

Introduce the unit on the value of responsibility by asking the students what responsibility means. Discuss the meaning of the song just played.

Say, "Today we will play with responsibility by having a trust walk." To do a trust walk, half the class wears blindfolds. One partner is responsible for carefully leading his or her blindfolded partner around, guiding physically as well as offering verbal information to manage uneven areas and to help the partner feel safe and comfortable. Do this for ten minutes, then reverse roles. Discuss the feelings associated with each role.

Ask: "How would you have felt if your partner were not responsible?"

RESPONSIBILITY LESSON 2
Responsible Guides

Discuss the following Reflection Point: Responsibility is accepting what is required and carrying out the task to the best of your ability.

Activity

Divide the students into teams of four. Three members of the team are to guide, only with words, the student whose eyes are covered. Suggest that the more responsible the guides are, the more easily the blindfolded person will navigate the path. Are we using our best ability to give accurate directions? Discuss the results and experiences.

—*Contributed by Pilar Quera Colomina*

RESPONSIBILITY LESSON 3
Responsibility Is "Walking My Talk"

Briefly ask the students the following questions:

Responsibility

- Do you believe in peace?
- What do you believe in? (Write peace and their other ideas on the board.)
- Do you believe in caring for the environment?
- Do you believe in loyalty?
- Do you believe in being a good friend?
- Do you believe in being a good student?

Say, "Responsibility means that you try your best to do what you believe in. Let's look at some of the Reflection Points."

♦ If we want peace, we have the responsibility to be peaceful.
♦ If we want a clean world, we have the responsibility to care for nature.
♦ With rights there are responsibilities.

Concept: One responsibility we sometimes overlook is doing what we say. If we believe in certain principles or values, then what we do or how we act should support our beliefs and values. "For instance, if I believe in caring for the environment, but I throw the candy wrapper on the ground, then I am not 'walking my talk.'"

Say, "Let's consider one of these." Make a separate heading for Caring for the Environment on the board. Ask: "If you believe in this, what type of behavior would you have? What would you do? . . . Good answers. Let's consider another one."

Activity

Ask students make an "I believe in . . ." booklet. At the top of each page, write one sentence starting with "I believe in . . ."

Down a few lines, write, "I want the right to . . ."

Down a few more lines, write, "My responsibilities are . . ."
Each student is to complete each sentence.

Say, "Each of us can create our own life. We can claim many
rights, but with those rights come responsibilities." Ask students
to share some of their "I believe in . . ." statements.

RESPONSIBILITY LESSON 4

Stories

Read folktales about responsibility to younger students. You
may have favorites or know of others of different cultures. A
story on responsibility for eight- to ten-year-olds is "TC Wants a
Dog." Discuss the story afterward, asking students how TC
proved to his mother that he was responsible. Ask: "How do you
show you are responsible?"

With older students, select works from the curriculum on
responsibility. Perhaps read current work on ecological responsibility, or whatever may be relevant to the students in your area.

RESPONSIBILITY LESSON 5

Sharing Tasks

"One basic definition of responsibility is doing your share.
When you were little you may have heard a story about a particular hen. Have you all heard that story? (Read it to the students if

Responsibility

it is available.) The hen wanted to have bread, but did not have any wheat. So she decided to plant some wheat. She asked someone to help, and he would not. At each step—when it came to watering the wheat, cutting it down, grinding the wheat, building a fire and making the bread—she continued to ask people if they wanted to help. Each time, no one did. But when it came to eating the bread, what happened? . . . That's right—everyone wanted to eat it! And she said, 'When I asked you to help me plant, water, harvest, grind and bake . . . you said no, no, no, no and no. And so, I made it myself and I'll eat it myself!'"

Say, "As humans, we are very lucky—we can create things— we do create our world. To be responsible, we have to do our share of a task. So what would you like to create? (Offer possible options in your setting. Offer something to do that is enjoyable.) Shall we start with a meal? Shall we start with a flower or vegetable garden?"

Ask students to choose, and then tell them to list materials needed and the tasks that need to be done. Suggest that teams accept responsibility for different tasks. For example, if you decide to make a Mexican or a Moroccan meal (because that is the cultural unit you are studying), one small group can work on decorations, another group on obtaining ingredients, etc.

Activity

In addition to a class responsibility activity, create the opportunity for each student to take up a responsibility at school. Perhaps three pairs of students can be conflict-resolution mediators at lunchtime for a week and another three pairs at recess. The next week, other students can take turns. Or perhaps some students would like to tutor, etc. Ask the students about tasks they would like to be responsible for. Be open to talking about their experiences and helping them generate solutions to any problems.

RESPONSIBILITY LESSON 6

My Responsibilities

Discuss/Share

- What responsibilities do you have to yourself?
- What responsibilities do you have as a student?
- What responsibilities do teachers have?
- Imagine a school where none of the teachers carried out any of their responsibilities. What would happen?
- How do you feel when you fulfill your responsibilities as a student?
- How do you feel and what are the consequences when you do not fulfill your responsibilities? Older groups of students might discuss the long-term results of this.
- What are your long-term goals? What would you like to do as an adult?

Discuss the following Reflection Point: Responsibility is not only something that obliges us, but also something that allows us to achieve what we wish.

Eight to Nine Activity: Instruct students to draw a picture of what they would like to do when they are adults. Ask them to write two things they can do now that will help them to accomplish that goal. Help them make these actions specific, practical

Responsibility

and immediate—something they can do within the next day or two. They should be small, observable actions. In this way, students can see when they are making progress toward their goal.

Ten to Fourteen Activity: Ask each student to choose one subject he or she would like to improve in. On a scale of one to ten—ten being the highest—how do they rate themselves? Instruct the students to think about something they can do to improve in that subject to get nearer their goal. The students can form pairs to talk this over. Their new behaviors should be specific, practical and easily observable. In this way, students can see when they are making progress toward their goal. Ask the students to write down three concrete things they can do. In three days, ask students in each pair to review their progress, and encourage students to continue working toward their goal.

Lesson 7

RESPONSIBILITY LESSON 7

Responsibilities in the Home

Discuss/Share

- What responsibilities do mothers have?
- What responsibilities do fathers have?
- What happens when parents do not fulfill their responsibilities?
- What kind of parent will you be when you are an adult?
- What responsibilities will be important to you?
- What responsibilities do you have as a son or daughter?
- What contributions do you make to your family?
- What contributions do you feel proud of?

Responsibility

Write the following Reflection Points on the board and discuss them with the students if you wish:

♦ Responsibility is accepting what is required and carrying out the task to the best of your ability.
♦ When one is responsible, there is the contentment of having made a contribution.

Eight to Nine Activity: Instruct the students to make a poem or write a card to their mother and/or father.

Ten to Fourteen Activity: Ask the students to reflect on the following questions and write a personal journal or a short essay on their reflections.

• What do you do that shows your mother you are responsible?
• Would you like to do anything else to show her your responsibility?
• What do you do that shows your father you are responsible?
• Would you like to do anything else to show him your responsibility?

RESPONSIBILITY LESSON 8
Story—"The Forgotten Garden"

Lesson
8

Read "The Forgotten Garden" story in the Appendix.

Eight-Year-Old Activity: Discuss the story and instruct the students to draw a picture of the garden.

Nine to Fourteen Activity: Discuss the story, and then ask:

Responsibility

- How do you feel when you do not do something you thought you should do?
- What kinds of things do you feel a little bad about if you don't do?
- What kinds of things do you feel very bad about?
- Is it important to feel bad? (Answer: Say, "Sometimes feeling bad is the way people know that it would be better to act in a different way. We all make mistakes sometimes. We are all human. But feeling bad a lot does not help us do the positive things we really want to do.")

Say, "Feeling sad or ashamed about something is natural, but it is not good to remain feeling like that. Instead:

1. Think about what you wish you would have done.
2. Identify the value or quality you need for that.
3. Imagine that quality and feel it in your mind.
4. Talk kindly to yourself. Know that the next time that circumstance occurs, you will have the power to do what you want to do."

Eleven to Fourteen Activity: Write the four steps on the board. Ask the students to write a personal essay, applying those four steps to a situation they would like to change. The teacher can ask the students to share, if they wish, kind things that one can say to oneself.

RESPONSIBILITY LESSON 9
Global Responsibility

Discuss the following Reflection Points:

♦ Global responsibility requires respect toward all human beings.

♦ Responsibility is using our resources to generate a positive change.

♦ A responsible person knows how to be fair, seeing that each gets a share.

Ask:

• If you could tell every person in the world that he or she had to be responsible, in what ways would you want people to be responsible?

• What would you want them to do?

• What would you want them not to do?

• What is our global responsibility?

• What is our societal responsibility?

• What is our moral responsibility? (thirteen- and fourteen-year-olds only)

Positively affirm the positive responses. Lead them in the Peace Relaxation exercise if that seems appropriate. This discussion will evoke a variety of reactions from different people. Older students may want to discuss these questions for several periods. Help them select relevant reading materials.

Responsibility

Activity

Instruct the students to make a Mind Map of responsibility in groups of two to four.

RESPONSIBILITY LESSON 10

Irresponsibility

Ask the students to discuss: "What would the world be like if no one carried out his or her responsibilities?"

Activity

Instruct the students to make a Mind Map of irresponsibility. The students can share their Mind Maps of irresponsibility and then their Mind Maps of responsibility from the prior lesson.

RESPONSIBILITY LESSON 11

My Responsibilities

Discuss the following Reflection Points:

♦ Each person can perceive his or her own world and look for the balance of rights and responsibilities.

♦ Responsibility is carrying out duties with integrity.

♦ As a responsible person, I have something worthwhile to offer—so do others.

Then ask:

- As a person, what responsibilities do you have to others?
- To society?

Activity

Ask the students to make a list of all the responsible actions the class has been discussing during the last week and to number each one. Ask each student to mark each act he or she believes in. Then ask each student to look at the list and circle the number if he or she does that action in an automatic way. Compare the lists and see if you would like to be more committed in action to the things you believe in.

—Contributed by Sabine Levy

RESPONSIBILITY LESSON 12

Taking Responsibility Makes Us a Good Friend

Lesson
12

Say, "To be responsible means that you are trustworthy. We all want our family to be responsible for us. The parents are responsible for providing food and shelter. As a child, I felt my parents were responsible for giving me love. A friend has the responsibility to be trustworthy."

Discuss

- How do I feel when people do not do what they say they will do or are irresponsible?

Responsibility

- How do you feel when your friend gossips about you or lets you down?
- How do you feel when your friend is trustworthy?
- What can we say to people when they are irresponsible or let us down?

Activity

Ask the students to form groups of five. Each student in the group is to generate two situations in which he or she feels someone has let him or her down or has been irresponsible in some way. They are to role-play those situations, coming up with two solutions for each problem. Discuss the consequences of each. When students discuss real problems they are confronting, allow them to create Situation Cards and continue discussing, role-playing, and generating positive, appropriate solutions.

Lesson 13

RESPONSIBILITY LESSON 13

I Believe

Activity

Do the Peace Relaxation/Focusing exercise with the students, and ask them to create an image of what they believe in. Below the image, each one is to write two new ways of being responsible. Make a collage on the wall.

RESPONSIBILITY LESSON 14
A Play

Activity

Divide the students into groups of eight to ten and ask them to make a play demonstrating irresponsibility and/or responsibility. It can be a comedy or a drama.

RESPONSIBILITY LESSON 15
A Program

Make plans in a group for a special program on what you have learned about two values. Decide who will be responsible for each area of the program.

Optional Activity For Students Ages 13–14

Explore responsibility through the regular curriculum. For example, learn about the different governing roles, public service, the functioning of associations or the content of the Convention on the Rights of the Child.

—Contributed by Pilar Quera Colomina and Sabine Levy

Responsibility

SEVEN

Cooperation

7. COOPERATION UNIT

COOPERATION LESSONS

159

Cooperation Reflection Points

♦ Cooperation exists when people work together toward a common goal.

♦ Cooperation requires recognizing the value of everyone's part and keeping a positive attitude.

♦ One who cooperates creates good wishes and pure feelings for others and the task.

♦ When cooperating, there is a need to know what is needed. Sometimes an idea is needed, sometimes we need to let go of our idea. Sometimes we need to lead and sometimes we need to follow.

♦ Cooperation is governed by the principle of mutual respect.

♦ One who cooperates receives cooperation.

♦ Where there is love, there is cooperation.

♦ By staying aware of my values, I can give cooperation.

♦ Courage, consideration, caring and sharing provide a foundation for cooperation.

Cooperation Unit

GOAL: To enjoy experiencing cooperation.
OBJECTIVES:

❏ To enjoy playing several cooperative games.
❏ To participate in a dance demonstrating cooperation.

GOAL: To increase knowledge about cooperation.

OBJECTIVES:

❏ To participate in discussions about the Cooperation Reflection Points and be able to talk about two or more.

❏ To discuss what words and behaviors contribute to playing and working together cooperatively.

❏ To create rules for good communication.

❏ To identify the values being used in a cooperative activity.

❏ To discuss sincere and insincere cooperation and to develop a skit on that theme.

❏ To Mind Map cooperation.

GOAL: To develop cooperative skills and participate cooperatively in activities.

OBJECTIVES:

❏ To positively acknowledge the cooperative efforts of other students.

❏ To participate in a cooperative project with the class.

❏ To create a game in a cooperative manner with a small group.

❏ To participate in helping and/or being helped at a Cooperation Table.

Cooperation Lessons

Add to the aforementioned list of Reflection Points using favorite sayings from your culture, from legends or quotes from respected individuals.

Continue to play a song daily.

Do one of the Relaxation/Focusing Exercises every day
or every several days, as suitable for your class. The students
may enjoy making up their own exercises.

COOPERATION LESSON 1

Cooperation Is Important

With younger students, explain that cooperation is important
because we can't do everything alone. Cooperation is helping to
achieve a task or a goal. (Ask older students why cooperation is
important.) Provide examples to which the students can relate. For
instance: "Suppose Sam has a car stuck in the mud and can't get
it out alone. Do you think all of us could get it out if we cooper-
ated? Or what if I decide I want all the furniture out of this room
within five minutes? I would need your cooperation. Suppose you
want to gain weight. You might need the cooperation of your
mother to buy foods which are high in fat content and calories."

We all need cooperation sometimes. Ask:

- What do you need cooperation with?
- What would you like more cooperation with?
- How do you feel about the task when the person helping is
  happy to help and when the person helping is grumpy or
  angry?

Point out that real cooperation is working together with
patience and affection—happily.

Cooperation

Cooperative Eating

Say, "Today we're going to have a snack (or lunch) that shows how important cooperation is. I want you all to pretend that your elbows do not work. They cannot bend. You have to figure out how to eat without bending your elbows! How are you going to do that?"

Allow the students to figure it out for themselves. For younger classes, teachers may need to model keeping their arms straight while someone gives them food. This activity should provide a lot of laughter while learning!

COOPERATION LESSON 2

Cooperative Playing

Lesson
2

Game: Play a song and ask the students to stand and form a circle, facing outside and linking arms at the elbows. Then ask them to sit down and to stand up again while keeping their arms linked and not breaking the circle. Ask them to repeat it a couple more times, doing it faster each time. In many cultures, girls and boys will need to form separate circles.

Game: With a ribbon, tie together the ankles of two or three students. Provide a balloon or a ball and instruct them to toss it back and forth among themselves. Then instruct them to toss it back and forth with another team that is tied at the ankles. The object of the game is for the teams to toss the ball back and forth as many times as they can without dropping it. If the teams are falling frequently, call "time out" for a few minutes so that team members can talk about what kind of cooperation would help them remain upright and able to toss the ball successfully. (Or, instead of tying the ankles together, teachers may elect to instruct the students to hold one long ribbon with their hands, not letting go as they play.)

Discuss the following Reflection Points:

♦ Cooperation exists when people work together toward a common goal.

♦ Cooperation requires recognizing the value of everyone's part and keeping a positive attitude.

♦ Cooperation is governed by the principle of mutual respect.

Ask what types of words and actions helped create a co-operative atmosphere during the game. If there are lots of ideas on increasing cooperation, try it again on another day.

Lesson 3

COOPERATION LESSON 3

Cooperation Table

Consider setting up a Cooperation Table in the classroom. Allow the students to decide what type of cooperation they want available. Examples include help with problems, special materials, compliments or encouragement on their work. The students can decide (within the parameters of time the teacher sets) who would be at the Cooperation Table and when. They can take turns at the table. For instance, the student who gets highest grades in math could be at the table for ten minutes after the teacher's lesson on mathematics. Good readers or writers could be available during part of the language arts period, and others could volunteer to tutor for exams for one period a day. The educator may wish to arrange for each student to be a "helper" at some point in time. Perhaps a student who does not have good academic skills can be part of the organizational or supply team, can teach games, juggling or crafts, or can help with sports. Continue the Cooperation Table for a couple of weeks or longer.

The price of using the Cooperation Table is a thank you to the cooperator for her or his cooperation. The cooperator, of course, would respond in a pleasant manner. Examples of responses include "You did a good job," "You have a good eye for detail," or "You listened and learned so well, it was a pleasure cooperating with you."

COOPERATION LESSON 4

Games

Game: Ask students to stand around the edges of a bed-sheet. Put a lightweight ball or an inflatable globe inside. Challenge the students to see if they can toss the ball up and catch it ten times in a row. Discuss afterward the various roles they played in order to accomplish the task. (Perhaps one became a leader and called out, "Up, down." Perhaps another was an "encourager." Maybe someone else was a willing and cooperative team player.)

Discuss the Reflection Point: Cooperation requires recognizing the value of everyone's part and keeping a positive attitude.

Then allow groups of students to gather in accordance with the sports they like. Students who play basketball can talk about the kinds of cooperation they want from each other. Students who play soccer can discuss what types of cooperation would improve their game.

Cooperation

Lesson 5

COOPERATION LESSON 5

Stories

Eight to Ten Activity: Read "A Meteorite Storm Approaches" in the Appendix. Discuss the story, and then ask the students to form groups of three and make up a story about cooperation. Draw a picture about your story.

A cute story by a third-grade group of students in Mauritius was about two frogs that got caught in a large pan of milk. They swam and swam. One frog wanted to quit, but the other frog kept encouraging him to continue to swim. So they both kept swimming, but it seemed even harder to swim. The milk soon tuned into butter, and they were able to jump out of the pan! The frogs agreed they could not have done it alone.

Eleven to Fourteen Activity: Read short stories or books about cooperation. There are many great human ventures that have required cooperation. Select one from your culture or from other cultures in your community.

In the story read, ask if there was evidence of the Reflection Point: One who cooperates receives cooperation? Ask if anyone has experienced this to be true. Ask for examples.

Lesson 6

COOPERATION LESSON 6

Game of Cooperation: The Star

Activity: Form groups of six to eight students. Ask the students to stand in a circle, join hands and balance themselves with their

Cooperation

legs one foot apart. Instruct the students to count off "one, two, one, two." With everyone keeping their feet where they are, the "ones" are to move forward and the "twos" backward, leaning until all achieve a point of balance. Once they achieve that point of balance, they are to change the direction of "falling."

After the game, reflect on the difficulties that emerged. Ask them to discuss: How did we achieve this cooperation? How did we feel? What helped? Reinforce the climate of dialogue and listening to each other.

Note: If time remains, begin with the next lesson.

—Contributed by Pilar Quera Colomina

COOPERATION LESSON 7

Create-a-Game

Lesson
7

Activity

Students can work in groups of three to create an educational board game for their peers or younger students. Ask them to brainstorm ideas and to design and make the board.

Example: Quest for Respect

A Snakes and Ladders type board could be created. Shake a die and move forward the number of spaces indicated. Certain squares would require the player to take a card and follow the instruction. Examples of instructions are: 1. Your friend asks you to lie to your mother. You say "No." Move forward three spaces.

Cooperation

2. Your best friend says she doesn't like your new dress, so you go home and change. Go back four spaces.

—Contributed by Ruth Liddle

Lesson 8

COOPERATION LESSON 8

I Cooperate

Complete the following sentences:

I cooperate with the school when _____.
I cooperate with myself when _____.
_____ is an example of cooperation.
To _____ is necessary cooperation.

Form groups of four to discuss your answers. Together create a slogan on cooperation. Draw or paint your slogan on a long piece of paper. Post it on the wall.

—Contributed by Marcia Maria Lins de Medeiros

Lesson 9

COOPERATION LESSON 9

Team Cooperation

Give one ruler, yardstick or meter to each group of five students. Ask them to measure the length of the playground accurately and quickly, using a team approach and accomplishing the task in the spirit of cooperation. Give the teams five minutes to discuss their approach, and then the game is on!

Cooperation

Later, the class can discuss what helped and what hindered the team effort. Ask the students to positively acknowledge cooperative efforts of each other. What values did they see being used?

COOPERATION LESSON 10

Good Communication

Activity

Ask the students to think about the cooperative project and the games the class has been doing and to create rules for good communication in small groups as a class. Write them out and post them on the wall so that they can be used, and perhaps expanded or improved upon, in subsequent sessions.

—Contributed by Sabine Levy

COOPERATION LESSON 11

A Skit

Discuss the concept of true cooperation—that is, cooperation given with affection, a sincere attitude and good wishes. Consider the Reflection Point: Where there is love, there is cooperation. Discuss how you can tell if there is insincere cooperation.

Activity

Ask groups of students to develop a skit about insincere cooperation versus true cooperation. It can be a humorous play.

COOPERATION LESSON 12
A Cooperative Project

Discuss the following Reflection Points:

♦ When cooperating, there is a need to know what is needed. Sometimes an idea is needed, sometimes we need to let go of our idea. Sometimes we need to lead and sometimes we need to follow.

♦ Courage, consideration, caring and sharing provide a foundation for cooperation.

♦ Cooperation requires recognizing the value of everyone's part and keeping a positive attitude.

♦ One who cooperates creates good wishes and pure feelings for others and the task.

Activity

Apply the principles of true cooperation to a project that the class would like to do—perhaps within the classroom. Examples are: making a cozy reading corner and agreeing to take turns using it and keeping it neat; working together to make one big mural of their vision of a better world; deciding to take a theme from the year's curriculum and to decorate the room in that theme. For example, a unit on the rain forest could develop into hanging jungle vines all across the room with parrots and monkeys, etc. Or a cooperative project could be planning and carrying out a car wash to earn money to take a field trip. Another type of venture would be identifying a need in the school or community and planning to help with that. These might include cooperating with a couple of other classes to keep the school ground clean, to work with a parent group to paint and fix up the playground equipment, or to read and help younger students on a rotating basis.

A cooperative project may take several days. As the students discuss and work together, reinforce the positive social skills that create harmony and cohesion in working together. Focus on the Cooperation Reflection Points as needed.

COOPERATION LESSON 13

Cooperation Needs Which Value?

Lesson

13

Discuss the following Reflection Point: By staying aware of my values, I can give cooperation. Then ask:

- What value is most important for cooperation?
- What value did you need most in our cooperative project? (It may be a different value for different students.)

Activity

Divide the class into groups, and ask them to choose among the different values the one that they think is most important for cooperation. Each group is to discuss the topic, agree on one value and then present that value to the entire class through mime.

—*Contributed by Marcia Maria Lins de Medeiros*

Cooperation

COOPERATION LESSON 14
Cooperative Mind Maps

Ask students to form groups of three and make a Mind Map of a country in which there is complete cooperation. They are to practice their best cooperative skills as they do so. Students can share their Mind Maps and display them.

COOPERATION LESSON 15
Cartoon

Create a cartoon in which the characters cooperate to contribute to a better world. Or write a story about cooperation.

—*Contributed by Marcia Maria Lins de Medeiros*

COOPERATION LESSON 16
Dance

Divide the class into three groups and ask them to demonstrate the spirit of cooperation through dance. They should select their own music.

Optional Activity for Older Students

Address different world problems and discuss cooperative ventures to resolve them. For example, world hunger, malnutrition of children or violence. Small groups of students can chose their topic, study relevant institutions or related subjects and then present their ideas.

—*Contributed by Pilar Quera Colomina and Sabine Levy*

EIGHT

Humility

8. HUMILITY UNIT

Humility Reflection Points

♦ Humility is staying light and easy inside.

♦ Humility goes together with self-respect.

♦ Humility is when I know my strengths but don't brag or show off.

177

Humility

♦ Humility makes arrogance disappear.

♦ A humble person can stay happy inside while listening to others.

♦ With the balance of self-respect and humility, I can stay powerful inside and not need to control others around me.

♦ Humility allows one to be great in the hearts of many.

♦ Humility creates an open mind.

♦ With humility I can recognize my own strengths and the strengths of others.

Humility Unit

GOAL: To increase knowledge about humility and its opposite.

OBJECTIVES:

❏ To participate in discussions about the Humility Reflection Points and be able to talk about two or more of them.

❏ To identify voice tones and behavior showing arrogance, and to participate in a discussion about how they feel when people brag.

❏ To participate in a discussion about the effects of feeling superior to others.

❏ To discuss the relationship between humility and love, and arrogance and lack of love.

❏ To write a poem about humility.

GOAL: To learn about the balance of self-respect and humility.

OBJECTIVES:

❏ To think about heroes who have the balance of humility and self-respect and to enact what they would say.

❏ To tell another student three things they are good at, first with confidence and humility and then in a bragging tone, and to discuss the difference.

❏ To interview someone from their neighborhood who had a positive impact on their life, and to discover what they are most proud of.

❏ To read stories about legends or historical figures who were humble and great.

❏ To create a personal symbol of the balance of humility and self-respect.

GOAL: To practice social skills with the aim of experiencing the balance of humility and self-respect.

OBJECTIVES:

❏ To do several nice things for others with the feeling of wanting to help and without needing praise.

❏ To practice enjoying seeing other people's strengths while accepting their own strengths.

Humility Lessons

Add to the above list of Reflection Points using favorite sayings from your culture, from legends or quotes from respected individuals.

Humility

Continue to play a song daily.

Do one of the Relaxation/Focusing exercises every day
or every several days, as suitable for your class. The students
may enjoy making up their own exercises.

Lesson
1

HUMILITY LESSON 1

Heroes with Humility

Concept: An interesting way to introduce the value of humility is
to talk about the humility of superheroes. Humility as taught in
these activities means a lack of arrogance. Inherent in the concept
is that humility goes hand-in-hand with self-respect and confidence.

Reflection Points that are useful to define humility are:

♦ Humility is staying light and easy inside.

♦ Humility goes together with self-respect.

♦ Humility is when I know my strengths but don't brag or
  show off.

Explain: Some superheroes are very good at the balance
between humility and self-respect. The teacher can illustrate this
concept, using as an example one of his or her heroes who has
the accurate balance between humility and self-respect.

Activity

Ask students to pick one of their favorite people or characters
who has the balance of self-respect and humility. These could be
famous historical figures, scientists, actors or superheroes or
heroines.

Humility

Ask students to think of a few comments the character might make if asked to remark about what particular personal aspect he or she is most proud of (or about what particular event he or she is most proud of).

Ask students to draw a picture of their character and make four or five "thought balloons" of comments the character might say.

HUMILITY LESSON 2

Heroes Speak

Discuss/Share

- How do you feel when someone is bragging about himself or herself?
- What do you know about someone who is always bragging? (That he or she does not have very much self-respect.)
- How do you feel about people who do many wonderful things, yet don't speak arrogantly about what they do?
- Can anybody demonstrate what an arrogant manner is? (If no one wishes to demonstrate, perhaps the teacher can!)
- Can anyone demonstrate a manner of self-respect and humility combined?
- What do you think about the following Reflection Point: Humility allows one to be great in the hearts of many?

Ask students to share their pictures. Ask a few to model how their hero would say what is in the thought balloon. Instruct them to first say it with arrogance, and then to say it in the same manner as the hero, with self-respect and humility.

Humility

Practice: Ask students to pair up with a partner and pretend they are that character. Practice relating what they are proud of, demonstrating both confidence and humility. Perhaps a couple of students could illustrate for the whole class. They might want to demonstrate a bragging tone first, followed by the quiet confidence and easiness of humility. Ask for reactions to each tone.

Then say: "Now I want each of you to pair up with the person next to you and tell the other person three things that you are good at. Tell the other person with confidence, yet humility. Then tell them with a bragging tone.

How is it different?

Lesson 3

A Loving and Humble Heart

Read a story about someone who is arrogant or someone who is full of respect, humility and love. In the Appendix there is a skit written by students at West Kidlington School called "Fairy Story— A Play." This could be read, and the students could act it out. Or, they can make up their own skits.

Discuss the story after it is read. Ask:

- Did you notice in the "Fairy Story" that the arrogant princess seemed only to have love for herself, while the princess who was loving and humble had love for everyone?
- Is there is a relation between humility and love, and arrogance and lack of love?

Humility

Discuss the following Reflection Point: Humility makes arrogance disappear.

Ask students to do something nice for someone at school every day for one week—with the feeling of wanting to help without needing praise. As the week progresses, ask: "Was it hard or easy?"

HUMILITY LESSON 4

Accepting an Award

Activity

Act out accepting an award as if you do not have humility, and then act it out with the balance of humility and self-respect. Ask a couple more students to pretend to give someone a gift with and without humility. Discuss the difference.

Discuss the proverb: Pride comes before a fall.

—*Contributed by Linda Heppenstall*

Twelve to Fourteen Additional Discussion: Think about the following Reflection Point: With the balance of self-respect and humility, I can stay powerful inside and not need to control others around me.

HUMILITY LESSON 5

The Perils of "Better Than"

After a song, begin with an analogy from nature. Say, "When we look at flowers in a garden or trees in a forest, they are all

Humility

different. You notice some are pretty in a certain way and others are pretty in another way, but you do not compare them. The flowers all contribute to the beauty of the garden.

"Very often, people who are arrogant go around trying to feel better than (superior to) other people." Ask:

- Why do you think they might want to do that? (So they can try to feel better about themselves.)

Say, "It is important to see the qualities of other people, and it is important to know the qualities you value in people. But to feel "better than" (superior to) creates problems." Ask:

- What kinds of problems can feeling "better than" others create?

List their responses on the board. Then ask:

- How would you like people to act or behave toward or think about each other?

Ask students if they would like to practice staying in the mindset of seeing and enjoying other people's strengths while accepting their own strengths.

Activity

Make up simple poems about humility and illustrate with a drawing. Examples are:

Humility protects me,
It's a gift.

Humility

With it I can sing,
And give everyone a lift!

Humility is great,
Humility is strong.
Under the protection of humility,
I can't go wrong!

HUMILITY LESSON 6
Interview

Think of someone from your neighborhood or community who has had a positive impact on your life. Interview that person and discover what they are most proud of. Write a story about that person or share about him or her in class.

HUMILITY LESSON 7
Story Time

With younger students, read folk tales and legends about people who were humble and great. With older students, read stories about historical figures who were humble and great—and who had a vision of benefit for the world.

HUMILITY LESSON 8

Staying Steady and Positive

Say, "Sometimes people start feeling bad inside when some-one else is telling them what wonderful things that person did." Ask: "Has that ever happened to any of you?"

Acknowledge: "Sometimes it is difficult to listen to so many wonderful things because we start to compare ourselves inside. Sometimes it is just that the other person is getting all the attention, and we want some attention, too. So today we are going to practice another skill, and this is how to stay in self-respect when listening to others. Humility is a big help in this."

Write the following Reflection Points on the board and discuss:

♦ A humble person can stay happy inside while listening to others.

♦ With humility I can recognize my own strengths and the strengths of others.

♦ Humility creates an open mind.

Ask students to think of three things they are proud of and to share those three things in a group of four people. The three other listeners are to practice feeling the balance of self-respect and humility. After the speaker's comments, they are to offer positive remarks, confirming those qualities the speaker may have mentioned or adding other qualities they notice in that individual.

Next, everyone in the small group takes a turn telling a story. Each one of the listeners is to listen carefully, repeating the part of the story she or he liked best when the storyteller is finished.

Or she or he can make a positive comment, such as, "Yes, it's great that you did that!"

Discuss/Share

Ask whether it was hard to resist trying to top the story. Inform the students that the tendency to want to "top a story" is a form of trying to be better than someone else. Make the point that confidence and humility together allow you to feel good inside and enjoy the other person's qualities also.

HUMILITY LESSON 9

Personal Symbol

Lesson
9

Ask the students what they learned during this unit on humility.

Activity

Create a personal symbol of the balance of self-respect and humility. Provide art materials.

End with the Change Place Game: The aim is for everyone to exchange positive statements and change seats. The teacher starts. For example, the teacher may say, "I'm going to change places with Troy because he is always smiling and that makes me feel good," or "I'm changing places with Patricia because she helped me out with a problem I had yesterday." The spoken-to student then does the same with someone else in the circle. Continue until each student has received a positive statement.

—Game contributed by Ruth Liddle

Humility

NINE

Honesty

9. HONESTY UNIT

Honesty Reflection Points

♦ Honesty is telling the truth.

♦ When I am honest, I feel clear inside.

Honesty

♦ A person worthy of confidence is honest and true.

♦ Honest thoughts, words and actions create harmony.

♦ Honesty is to use well what has been entrusted to you.

♦ Honesty is the best policy.

♦ There is a deep relationship between honesty and friendship.

♦ When I am honest, I can learn and help others learn to be giving.

♦ Greed is sometimes at the root of dishonesty.

♦ There is enough for man's need, but not enough for man's greed.

♦ When we are aware we are interconnected, we recognize the importance of honesty.

Honesty Unit

GOAL: To increase knowledge about honesty.
OBJECTIVES:

❏ To participate in discussions about the Honesty Reflection Points and be able to talk about two or more.

❏ To understand the relationship between honesty and trust.

GOAL: To develop awareness about the effects of dishonesty.
OBJECTIVES:

❏ To create and then participate in a skit on the theme of honesty and dishonesty, placed within a period of history the students have been studying, and to discuss the effects on the people of that time economically and socially.

❏ To Mind Map the effects of honesty or dishonesty in small groups, and to share their Mind Maps with other groups.

❑ To participate in lessons and discussions about why people lie, how we feel when we lie, how we feel about others when they lie and how others feel about us when we lie.

❑ For older students to examine the effects of dishonesty and corruption in a real world event.

GOAL: To learn social skills that can help one be honest.

OBJECTIVES:

❑ To participate in lessons about "one minute of courage."

❑ To discuss and practice communication skills when we have done something we regret.

❑ To make up Honesty Situation Cards and act out honest and dishonest responses and the consequences.

GOAL: To value being honest.

OBJECTIVES:

❑ To enjoy "The Emperor and the Flower Seed" story and be asked to think of a time when they were loved for their honesty.

❑ To understand that when I am honest, I will be clearer and happier inside.

❑ To write three guidelines for being a good friend.

Honesty Lessons

Continue to play a song daily.

Do one of the Relaxation/Focusing exercises every day or every several days, as suitable for your class. The students may enjoy making up their own exercises.

HONESTY LESSON 1
The Emperor and the Flower Seeds

Read "The Emperor and the Flower Seeds" in the Appendix.
Discuss the story, and then discuss it in relationship to the following Reflection Point: A person worthy of confidence is honest and true.

Activity

Ask younger students to draw a picture of one aspect of the tale, or make a few props in preparation for acting out the story during the next lesson. Older students could write a short story on why the Emperor chose the little girl.

Alternative Activity: Ask the students to think about and then discuss in pairs how they would rule their kingdom if they were a king or queen. They can then write some of their ideas.

HONESTY LESSON 2
Flower Seeds

Read "The Emperor and the Flower Seeds" story again, this time with the students acting out the story.

Discuss/Share

Begin with the comment that Serena, the protagonist, is loved for her honesty. Ask:

Honesty

- Can you think of a time when you were loved for your honesty?
- Who would like to share?
- Can you think of a time when you really appreciated someone else's honesty?

Activity

Write a short personal essay on, "I was loved for my honesty when _____," or, "I like people to be honest because _____."

HONESTY LESSON 3

A Drama

Ask the students to make up a skit, portraying the themes of honesty and dishonesty or cheating. The students could take the context from a unit the class has been studying, such as a stockbroker's office and investors, a feudal lord of medieval times, a current conflict in the world or a theme from a social studies unit. If you are working with a large group, divide into smaller groups. After the skits, the class can discuss the effects economically and socially. Ask:

- What was the effect on the people who were cheated?
- What is the effect of the dishonesty or greed on these people's lives?

Honesty

Ask the actors to add how they felt from a subjective standpoint.

Discuss the following Reflection Points:

♦ Greed is sometimes at the root of dishonesty.

♦ There is enough for man's need, but not enough for man's greed.

Twelve to Fourteen Homework: Ask students to bring in a story on honesty or corruption from the newspaper or radio. Or think about a historical example of corruption from a unit of history recently studied and be ready to discuss it during the next lesson.

NOTE TO TEACHER

Sometimes the students want to enact their skit again. If they do, allow each actor to have a "shadow," a person who speaks the actor's true feelings and responds to questions from the class about thoughts of the actor. An actor can have more than one shadow when other students have different ideas to share.

Lesson

4

HONESTY LESSON 4

Corruption

Eight to Eleven Activity: Allow the rest of the students to perform their skits from the last lesson. Mind Map the effects of dishonesty in a skit of their choice.

Twelve to Fourteen Activity: Ask students to share the stories of honesty or corruption they have gathered; or discuss a historical

Honesty

example of corruption from a unit of history recently studied. Discuss the effects on the person, other people and the effect on the general well-being of the country where the corruption occurs. Examine the short-term and long-term effects. Ask students to form small groups. Ask half the groups to Mind Map the results of dishonesty and the other half to Mind Map the results of honesty. Let them share and post their Mind Maps. (Two lesson periods may be needed to do this.)

HONESTY LESSON 5

One Minute of Courage

There are many classic tales of dishonesty. "Matilda" by Hilaire Belloc and "The Boy Who Cried Wolf" are about students who came to misfortune because of dishonesty. Teachers of older students may want to choose a real life story from the newspaper about a person who was ruined because of dishonesty (corruption). Tell a story about dishonesty and have a discussion.

Say, "This story was a dramatic example of what happened with a lie (dishonesty). Today let's talk more about lying and examine what happens when someone tells a lie."

Discuss

- How does it feel to be honest?
- Is honesty valued?
- How does it feel to be dishonest, if found out? If not found out?

Honesty

- Do you know an honest person?
- How do you feel about him or her?
- What are the consequences of dishonesty?
- What makes us dishonest?

—Contributed by Linda Heppenstall

Say, "Yes, occasionally people who tell a lie get away with it. But why do they lie in the first place? Usually people lie because they are afraid of being embarrassed, or they may try to avoid being punished for having done something wrong. Then, when they're trying to cover the lie, things get very complicated because they have to remember what they said and what they did not say." Ask:

- But what happens when people find out we lied? (They get angry with us.)

"Yes, that's right. They get even angrier and more disappointed, and we get into even more trouble. And although people may not look so clever sometimes, usually they can figure out the truth fairly well! And if we lie once, they may not trust us to tell the truth another time."

Ask: "How much energy does it takes to cover the lie versus telling the truth? It takes one minute of real courage to tell the truth."

Say, "The Reflection Point for today is: When I am honest, I feel clear inside. You may use this in your story if you wish."

Activity

Ask the class to write a short story using a real or imaginary situation in which a person lied. Or students can make up a poem.

Honesty

HONESTY LESSON 6
Babe

Watch the film *Babe*. This story about a brave, honest animal can be fun and will generate some interesting discussion. Or, show another film with an honesty character.

Application: Help the students to evaluate their own efforts. Honest self-evaluation is important and useful in making progress.

—Contributed by Pilar Quera Colomina

HONESTY LESSON 7
Trust

Discuss/Share

- How would you feel if a neighbor wanted you to wash his car and said he would give you _____  (give an appropriate amount of money for the age of the students and the country), but did not pay you when you finished?
- Was this man being honest? (No.)
- What do you think the man should have done?
- How would you feel if a person said she would pay you for picking fruit from her orchard, but then only paid you half of what she said?
- Was this woman being honest?

Say, "Part of honesty is keeping our word. Our societies run much better when people keep their word." Ask:

Honesty

- Can you think of other examples of people not keeping their word?
- Can you think of examples of people breaking their promises?
- How do you feel when people break their promises?
- Do you feel you can trust someone who keeps his or her word?
- Do you want people to trust you?
- Why?

"It's important to be honest because our relationships are then built on trust. When people are honest and trustworthy, we know we can depend on them."

"In the same way that it sometimes takes courage to tell the truth—like when we did something we weren't supposed to, or when we didn't do something we were supposed to—it also takes courage to apologize for not keeping a promise." Ask:

- If someone did not keep his or her promise to you, what would you like her or him to say?
- If you did not keep your promise to someone, what could you say? Please start your sentence with "I" and share your feelings.

With older students, ask them to use the previously presented communication skill of: "I feel _____ when _____ because _____." For example, "I felt bad when I was late because I let you down and I really value your friendship."

In groups of two, think of three different situations and practice using the above skill.

Honesty

HONESTY LESSON 8

Lost and Found

Discuss/Share

- How would you feel if you lost your favorite game/toy? (Use the name of an object appropriate for the age of the students.)
- How would you feel if someone found your game and returned it to you?
- How would you feel if you lost your lunch money (or something equivalent)?
- How would you feel if someone saw you drop it and returned it to you?
- How would you feel if we all worked very hard and then someone stole all our money?

Acknowledge their feelings and responses. Acknowledge that it is not kind for someone to do that.

Say, "Some people are not honest. Some people are very greedy. What do greedy people say? They say, 'It's all for me! It's all mine!' and they take what belongs to others."

Say, "Let's imagine that you saw a friend drop some money. You pick up the money quickly, and run up to her and give it to her." Ask:

- What does she say?
- How do you feel?

Honesty

Say, "Let's imagine that you saw a friend drop some money. You pick up the money quickly, and then run the other way." Ask:

- How do you feel?
- How do you feel after one hour?
- How do you feel after one day?
- What can you do about it?

Say, "An interesting thing about human beings is that when we do something good, we automatically feel happy inside. When we do something wrong, we may try to justify it to ourselves—but we still feel bad because we cannot really fool ourselves inside for very long."

Discuss the following Reflection Points:

♦ When I feel honest, I feel clear inside.
♦ When I am honest, I can learn and help others learn to be giving.

Activity

Make up a skit about someone who is dishonest and someone who is honest.

Lesson
9

HONESTY LESSON 9

The Miner and the Prince

Honesty

Read the story "The Miner and the Prince" in the Appendix. Discuss the story and its implications. Then say, "Sometimes there is pressure to be dishonest." Ask:

• Can you think of any examples?

Say, "Sometimes it is difficult to resist that pressure." Ask:

• What things can you think of that would help you resist the pressure to _____.
(Insert one of the examples the students gave you. It might be about lying, cheating, stealing, etc.)

• What kinds of things could you say to yourself or to a friend if there is a temptation to be dishonest?

• Would it help you resist the temptation if you looked at the consequences? What could happen as a result? (Teachers might want to question further about consequences, such as the feelings over time of the one who has cheated, the effect on relationships with friends, trust and loss of trust, hurt or harm to others, belief in the self, etc.)

Eight to Nine Activity: Draw your favorite scene from "The Miner and the Prince," and below the picture write why you like that scene.

Ten to Fourteen Activity: Organize students into groups of four or six to make up a Situation Card on honesty. (There are blank Situation Cards in the Appendix.) Instruct each group to act out a situation, acting out the dishonest and honest responses and the consequences. The "actors" may freeze the skit at times to share their thoughts in an aside to the audience.

Honesty

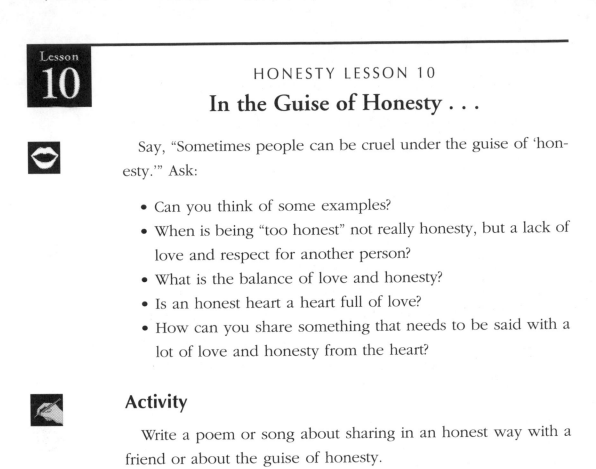

HONESTY LESSON 10

In the Guise of Honesty . . .

Say, "Sometimes people can be cruel under the guise of 'honesty.'" Ask:

- Can you think of some examples?
- When is being "too honest" not really honesty, but a lack of love and respect for another person?
- What is the balance of love and honesty?
- Is an honest heart a heart full of love?
- How can you share something that needs to be said with a lot of love and honesty from the heart?

Activity

Write a poem or song about sharing in an honest way with a friend or about the guise of honesty.

HONESTY LESSON 11

Honesty and Friendship

Discuss/Share

Highlight the following Honesty Reflection Point: There is a deep relationship between honesty and friendship. Ask the students to think about a friend who always tells the truth and keeps his or her promises. Ask:

- How do you feel about that person?
- How does that behavior affect your relationship?
- Have you experienced this Reflection Point: Honest thoughts, words, and actions create harmony?
- What makes a good friend?
- If you could write guidelines for being a good friend, what would you write?

Activity

Write three guidelines for being a good friend.

Honesty

TEN

Simplicity

10. SIMPLICITY UNIT

Simplicity

Simplicity Reflection Points

- ◆ Simplicity is natural. Simplicity is being natural.
- ◆ Simplicity is learning from the Earth.
- ◆ Simplicity is beautiful.
- ◆ Simplicity is relaxing.
- ◆ Simplicity is staying in the present and not making things complicated.
- ◆ Simplicity is enjoying a plain mind and intellect.
- ◆ Simplicity teaches us economy—how to use our resources wisely, keeping future generations in mind.
- ◆ Simplicity is giving patience, friendship and encouragement.
- ◆ Simplicity is appreciating the small things in life.

Simplicity Unit

GOAL: To increase knowledge about and enjoy simplicity.
OBJECTIVES:

- ❏ To participate in discussions about the Simplicity Reflection Points and be able to talk about two or more.
- ❏ To express simplicity artistically.
- ❏ To enjoy observing simple things in nature during a walk.
- ❏ To discuss and write about the simple things they enjoy.
- ❏ To write a class play about rediscovering the simple things in life/nature.
- ❏ To participate in class discussions about the message behind selected advertisements and be able to generate an alternate "simplicity is natural" message in response.

GOAL: To learn about the simple wisdom of native cultures.

OBJECTIVES:

❏ To learn several ways in which native cultures used resources wisely.

❏ To discuss the values within the cultural practices being studied.

GOAL: To learn about simplicity in caring for the environment.

OBJECTIVES:

❏ To learn about simplicity as the precursor to sustainable development.

❏ To think of ways to conserve in the classroom, and to carry out at least two of those actions.

❏ To do one environment-friendly project at the school.

❏ To use information being studied to carry out an environmental project in the community (for older students).

Simplicity Lessons

Teachers at the school or at the country level will need to select information from the curriculum or literary resources about the native peoples of the area. For younger students, storybooks about customs and children of that culture would be good. For older students, more factual information about customs and traditions would be excellent.

Add to the above list of Reflection Points using favorite sayings from your culture, from legends or quotes from respected individuals.

Simplicity

Continue to play a song daily.

Do one of the Relaxation/Focusing exercises every day or every several days, as suitable for your class. The students may enjoy making up their own exercises.

SIMPLICITY LESSON 1

Simple Art

Introduce the value of Simplicity and write the following Reflection Points on the board:

♦ Simplicity is natural. Simplicity is being natural.
♦ Simplicity is beautiful.

Activity

Explore works of art, historical pictures or magazines for examples of simplicity versus something gaudily or excessively adorned. Make a collage or picture that reflects simplicity. While the students are working, play a beautiful piece of music with a simple melody or a recording of the sounds of nature.

Or collect a few leaves and make a beautiful picture with those leaves. Paint them, draw them or place them under a piece of paper and color on top of them.

Native Simplicity

Purpose: To learn about and appreciate the native wisdom of your heritage and the heritage of others. In ancient traditions, natural simplicity, wisdom and respect for the Earth were inherent in almost every practice. The needs of the people and the methods to satisfy those needs were simple and without waste. Look at the natural simplicity in the lives of your country's native peoples. Discover ways in which native peoples have used resources by reading a story, visiting a museum or a library with an exhibit, or viewing a film. Invite members of the community who can share artifacts or crafts from your heritage.

At some time during your lessons on traditional wisdom, discuss the Reflection Points: Simplicity is learning from the Earth. Simplicity teaches us economy—how to use our resources wisely, keeping future generations in mind. Point out, or ask the students to explore, how the people of native cultures were wise in doing this. Ask them which values are inherent in different practices. Ask:

• Which aspects of their wisdom do you think it would be beneficial to practice in today's world?

Many native cultures in Africa, the Americas, Australia, Asia and the Pacific islands showed respect for the Earth and its resources in their gathering and hunting practices. For example, Native American Indian tribes were simple, economical and wise in their use of plants and natural resources. Indians in the deserts

Simplicity

of what is now California used each part of the ocotillo plant—the roots, leaves and stem. They never overused resources and thus guaranteed there would be plenty. The Gwich'in Indians in the far north considered caribou reindeer to be their brothers. From the caribou, they made food, clothing, snowshoes, cooking vessels and houses. The Indians considered themselves to be rich, as they were warm, were well fed, and had plenty of time for their arts and prayers.

Ask students to draw and write about the results of their investigation. The class could do an art project, duplicating something from their heritage. Or they could make a clay model and tell their parents about it when they bring it home. In preparation for the "at-home presentation," ask students to tell you their points about the object and its history. Tell them to write their points on the board and to practice with a peer partner before they take the object home.

Lesson 3

SIMPLICITY LESSON 3—FOR A WEEK OR MORE
Conservation, Respect for the Earth

Concept: Simplicity is the precursor to sustainable development. Simplicity teaches us economy—how to use our resources with the needs of future generations in mind. When we, as students, learn to respect the Earth, we will, as adults, respect the Earth. Simple methods can be effective in achieving a goal.

Activity

The teacher may want to begin this exercise by showing a film about the Earth or reading another story about a tradition that held great love for Mother Earth. Or ask the students why we should respect and take care of the Earth. (They often have the best answers!) Talk about simplicity as the precursor to sustainable development. Follow this by asking the students to think of ideas or ways to conserve in the classroom. For example, they could set up a recycling bin, they could use paper on both sides, and everyone could save magazines and little sticks to be used for art projects. They may decide to generate ideas about how to be careful about not wasting water.

Activity

On the school grounds, they could pick up litter or plant trees and bushes. They could research environmental concerns to do with the school. They could question whether we are polluting or wasting our water. For instance, if the grass is being watered in the afternoon, they could ask the school principal to change the watering schedule from the afternoon to the morning to conserve water.

Activity

After the students have thought about and implemented a few respect-for-the-Earth changes, ask them to generate ideas for the home or the community. If litter or waste is affecting the clean water supply, address that issue. Perhaps help clean up a local river. Some students may want to research local usage of pesticides and natural (and cheaper) alternatives that do not pollute

Simplicity

the Earth or its inhabitants. They could write to their local mayor sharing their ideas. They could make up respect-for-the-Earth slogans and post them at school and at sports-game locales in the community.

Think about: "A lot of the good we do, no one knows about. But it is real. You could be a secret Earth Helper. When you are walking by yourself and enjoying nature, sometimes there's a chance to give a little back to Mother Earth. Pick up litter, walk around a little flower that is starting to spring up from the soil, gently help an insect which is stuck in a pool of water."

Lesson 4

SIMPLICITY LESSON 4

Story

One story that ties in well with the theme of simplicity is "The Precious Present" by Spencer Johnson. After the students read it, ask them to write about what they learned and to draw a picture about their story. Attach the stories to the pictures and form a big book of lessons learned.

"The Precious Present" is a simple story about someone who knows when we stay in the present moment, we are free to enjoy it and be nourished by it. We are free from guilt from the past and worry for the future. The story relates well to the following Simplicity Reflection Points:

♦ Simplicity is staying in the present and not making things complicated.
♦ Simplicity is enjoying a plain mind and intellect.

SIMPLICITY LESSON 5

A Nature Walk

A nature walk easily offers the experience of the following Simplicity Reflection Points:

♦ Simplicity is natural.
♦ Simplicity is beautiful.
♦ Simplicity is relaxing.
♦ Simplicity is appreciating the small things in life.

Activity

Take a walk in a nearby park or go on a field trip to a botanical garden or the seashore. For fifteen minutes of your time there, walk in silence. Observe the simple things: the light on the leaf, a tree, a small flower, a bird or whatever element of nature you notice. Lie under a tree and watch the leaves. For a few minutes, simply be an observer, free from desires.

When you return, write a poem as though it were from part of nature. For example, a poem from the tree to you, a poem from the bird to the class, or . . . ?

Homework: Give the students Simplicity-Is-Relaxing and Simplicity-Is-Not-Making-Things-Complicated homework. Ask them to spend five minutes every day for one week relaxing. They may wish to focus on a tree, a flower or a light. Focus on the beauty of what is natural. Know that the natural you is beautiful.

Simplicity

Lesson 6

SIMPLICITY LESSON 6
Enjoying Simple Things

Discuss/Share

Say, "Think for a moment of a time when you enjoyed something that you could not buy in a shop." Ask:

- What are the simple things you enjoy?
- How often have you said you were bored?
- Was it you that were bored or the things around you that were boring?
- How did our grandparents entertain themselves before TV?

Activity

Sentence completion:

I find life too complicated when . . .

I can calm myself down by . . .

Form pairs to discuss a simple pleasure you both enjoy and what you think about in quiet moments. Report to the class.

—Contributed by Linda Heppenstall

Lesson 7

SIMPLICITY LESSON 7
Express

Draw simplicity, dance simplicity.

Simplicity

SIMPLICITY LESSON 8

Simplicity Is Being Natural, Simplicity Is Beautiful

Concept: Appreciating the beauty of nature and the Earth sometimes allows us to appreciate the natural beauty of the self more. The more we appreciate natural beauty, the less we are fooled into thinking we have to own certain things or look a certain way to feel good about ourselves or be accepted by others. In order to sell things, businesses hire advertising firms to create impressive advertisements so people buy their products. Sometimes they imply that you will be more attractive if you use their product or feel better about yourself if you own what they are selling. These advertisements fool people into thinking they need these things to be okay and for other people to consider them okay. When people hear many messages like this, they often forget about the importance of inner beauty. These messages do not encourage people to respect the Earth or the inner self. The self knows there is natural beauty inside. When we have that awareness in our own mind, we can be content about our own value, enjoy others for who they are, and give happiness. Simplicity is being natural. Simplicity is beautiful.

Activity

Share this concept with the students and ask them to brainstorm messages they get from the mass media and from advertisements. List those messages on the board. Choose one of the

Simplicity

messages and ask them to discuss that. Then make another list, and ask them to create thoughts they think are closer to nature and natural beauty. Take another example and repeat. Keep a list of their examples.

SIMPLICITY LESSON 9

What Is the Real Message?

Discuss the following Reflection Point with students ages eleven through fourteen:

Simplicity asks whether we are being induced to purchase unnecessary products. Psychological enticements create artificial needs. Desires stimulated by wanting unnecessary things result in value clashes complicated by greed, fear, peer pressure and a false sense of identify. Once fulfillment of basic necessities allow for a comfortable lifestyles, extremes and excesses invite overindulgence and waste.

Activity

Continue the same activity as the last lesson, choosing another message and going through the same process. The students can bring in advertisements.

Homework: For one week, ask everyone to experiment with simplicity by wearing simple clothes to school or when out with friends. Say you would like them to remember to keep in mind the following simplicity points: Simplicity is being natural. Simplicity is beautiful.

Activity

At the end of the week, ask for their feelings and reactions. Ask them to write a short essay on their experience.

SIMPLICITY LESSON 10

Freedom from Desires

Lesson
10

Discuss the following Reflection Points offered by students at West Kidlington School:

♦ Simplicity is freedom from material desires and emotional desires—permission to simply "be."
♦ Simplicity avoids waste, teaches economy, and avoids value clashes complicated by greed, fear, peer pressure, and a false sense of identity.
♦ From simplicity grow generosity and sharing.
♦ Simplicity is putting others first with kindness, openness, pure intentions—without expectations and conditions.

Include the following Reflection Point in your discussion:

♦ Simplicity is giving patience, friendship and encouragement.

Activity

List the above Reflection Points on the board. Ask the students to form small groups and discuss the points. Ask them to make up a slogan on simplicity that they would like to communicate to others. Allow them different options to decorate it.

Simplicity

SIMPLICITY LESSON 11
A Play

Activity

Write a class play about rediscovering the simple things in life/nature. Perhaps perform it for an assembly.

—*Contributed by Linda Heppenstall*

ELEVEN

Freedom

11. FREEDOM UNIT

Freedom

Freedom Reflection Points

- ♦ Freedom resides within the mind and heart.
- ♦ Freedom is a precious gift.
- ♦ There can be full freedom when rights are balanced with responsibilities.
- ♦ There is full freedom when everyone has equal rights.
- ♦ All people have a right to be free. For all to be free, each one has to respect the rights of others.
- ♦ Inner freedom is experienced when I have positive thoughts for all, including myself.

Freedom Unit

GOAL: To enjoy the feeling of inner freedom and learn about personal skills that contribute to that experience.

OBJECTIVES:

- ❏ To enjoy participating in a "Free Song."
- ❏ To participate in a discussion about freeing thoughts and constraining thoughts.
- ❏ To enjoy a Freedom Relaxation/Focusing exercise.
- ❏ To make a puppet or symbol of inner freedom.

GOAL: To increase knowledge about freedom.

OBJECTIVES:

- ❏ To participate in discussions about the Freedom Reflection Points and be able to talk about two or more.
- ❏ To identify the kinds of freedom we have now.
- ❏ To choose their favorite freedom quote or saying and orally state that in a circle activity.

❑ To discuss the concept, "For all to be free, each has to respect the rights of others."

❑ To discuss responsibilities in relationship to two or more rights.

❑ To participate in a conflict resolution process to create a better solution while considering the benefit for all.

GOAL: To learn about freedom in relation to history and the world.

OBJECTIVES:

❑ To enact a scene related to freedom from their country's or the world's history.

❑ To identify rights people have felt denied of in relation to a history lesson.

❑ To become familiar with some of the rights in the Universal Declaration of Human Rights.

❑ To create a list of rights which everyone could have that do not infringe on the rights of others.

Freedom Lessons

Add to the above list of Reflections Points using favorite sayings from your culture, from legends or quotes from respected individuals.

Continue to play a song daily.

Do one of the Relaxation/Focusing exercises every day or every several days, as suitable for your class. The students may enjoy making up their own exercises.

Freedom

Lesson 1

FREEDOM LESSON 1
Story

Eight to Eleven Activity: Read "The Naughty Little Prince" story in the Appendix.

Discuss the story, and then talk about it in relation to the following Reflection Points:

◆ All people have a right to be free. For all to be free, each one has to respect the rights of others.

◆ Inner freedom is experienced when I have positive thoughts for all, including myself.

Twelve to Fourteen Activity: Read a story or poem on freedom—one of your favorites, or one from the culture of the students or the curriculum.

Discuss the story or poem and discuss it in relation to the relevant Reflection Points.

Lesson 2

FREEDOM LESSON 2
A Slice of History

Groups of students can take a powerful slice of their country's or the world's history and enact a dramatic scene related to freedom. This can be done in conjunction with a relevant history or social studies lesson on slavery, independence, establishment of a new country, civil rights, etc. At relevant points during the regular social studies or history unit, generate discussion.

Freedom

- Identify the rights the people felt were denied to them.
- What kinds of freedom did they want?
- Why did they want those kinds of freedom?
- How did the group denying them those kinds of freedom benefit?

At the end of the history unit, divide the students into co-operative groups. Give the groups a couple sessions to develop a presentation: a skit, a song from each perspective or a poem. This will require more than one period of time.

Another lesson: After the skit (or presentation), the class can participate in further discussion about the freedoms those people desired. Ask:

- How did the people on each of the two sides feel?
- Which of these kinds of freedom do we have now?
- What other kinds of freedom do we have?
- What kinds of freedom do you think all people should have?

Follow-up activities:

Depending upon the age of the students, these latter questions can form themes for study, debate or essays.

Write a story or essay from the perspective of a historical character.

Write about what kinds of freedoms you want all people to have now.

Teams of students could plan and paint a freedom mural about the era of history they are studying.

Lesson 3

FREEDOM LESSON 3

Favorite Famous Freedom Lines

Ask students to choose their favorite famous sayings about freedom. For younger students, the teacher will want to select materials from which to chose. Folk tales on freedom could be read. They might choose a line from *The Universal Declaration of Human Rights—An Adaptation for Students,* or from *Living Values: A Guidebook.* Older students could browse the quote section of the Internet or Worldwide Web if that is available, or study the essays of their country's champions of freedom. The teacher may also use this material to help build vocabulary as well as to teach students new concepts.

Once students identify their favorite freedom line or quote about freedom, ask them to write a story about it, write a letter to the government about it or a make a journal entry on why they like that particular freedom.

As a concluding activity, ask the students to stand in a circle, each child stating his or her one-line quote. Go around the circle once more, asking each to repeat the root phrase, "I feel lucky I have the freedom to . . ." and to add his or her own statement. Or they can complete the sentence, "I wish all people had the freedom to . . . ."

Free song

Starting from common sounds, each one sings his/her own melody.

—Contributed by Dominique Ache

Freedom

FREEDOM LESSON 4

Inner Freedom

The teacher can explain that freedom is the state of being free. It is often used in the context of being free from a negative or constraining condition. The teacher may want to refer to a previous unit, saying that in history we studied a time when people were seeking freedom from oppression, from someone else ruling over them. There is also freedom from want. There is also something called inner freedom. Ask:

- What do you think inner freedom feels like?
- Are you then free from worry, free from thinking someone may not be your friend?
- When do you feel the most free?
- What types of thoughts make you feel free?
- What types of thoughts make you feel constrained or negative?

Write their contributions down on the board in two columns, one headed Freeing Thoughts, the other Constraining Thoughts. The teacher may want to contribute a few. Examples under Freeing Thoughts might be: I am a good person, I am capable and lovable, I have the freedom to choose what is in my mind, Love makes my heart feel free, etc. Examples under Constraining Thoughts might be: I won't be able to do this, I'll never understand this, etc.

Discuss the following Reflection Point: Freedom resides within the mind and heart.

Freedom

Do the Freedom Relaxation Exercise:

Say, "As I relax, I give my mind the freedom to explore. . . . I imagine that I'm flying through the air . . . like a bird . . . floating on the warm gusts of wind . . . effortlessly . . . feeling free and light. . . . I feel the warm rays of the sun on my back. . . . I am completely free. . . . I let go of any worries and feel light inside . . . no anchors, nothing to stop me . . . and so I fly into the future world . . . and there I find a world of freedom . . . where each person is free . . . content . . . happy. . . . I see students of all races playing together in complete harmony . . . having the freedom of being able to play . . . each respecting the space and time of the other people. . . . In this world, there is respect and love for each person . . . students feel free to make their own choices . . . everything is perfectly balanced. . . . With my mind free from worry, I fly back into the present . . . and I feel free to experience my inner self . . . to appreciate my inner beauty. . . . I am light inside."

—Based on a contribution by Sue Emery

FREEDOM LESSON 5

Symbols of Inner Freedom

Eight to Ten Activity: Instruct each student to make a puppet symbolizing inner freedom, perhaps a bird, a kite or a butterfly. Play music and suggest that their puppet move to what inner freedom feels like. Or create a puppet show on inner freedom.

Eleven to Fourteen Activity: Create the opportunity for each student to make a symbol of inner freedom. Ask them to write the thoughts that create that experience as part of their symbol.

—Contributed by Encarnación Royo Costa

Freedom

FREEDOM LESSON 6
Poetry

Discuss the Reflection Point: Inner freedom is experienced when I have positive thoughts for all, including myself.

Do the Freedom Relaxation Exercise again.

Activity

Write a poem on inner freedom or draw a picture. Some students may wish to contrast the state of being worried or feeling burdened versus the state of feeling free. Acknowledge their feelings.

FREEDOM LESSON 7
Artistic Expression

Discuss the Reflection Point: Freedom is a precious gift. Ask the students what kinds of freedom they have.

Play a song about freedom.

Activity

Groups of students could create a "living sculpture" or a dance expressing inner freedom. Or write poems or stories on "I believe in freedom because . . ."

Freedom

FREEDOM LESSON 8

Human Rights

Discuss the following Reflection Point: All people have a right to be free. For all to be free, each one has to respect the rights of others.

Study The Universal Declaration of Human Rights. An adaptation for students is recommended for students ages eight to eleven. This provides thoughtful text and illustrations. Whether or not this is available, ask the students what rights they think are important. Create a list of rights which everyone could have that do not infringe on the rights of others. If they come up with a "right" that would violate the rights of others, question them about the consequences. Ask them if this would violate the rights of others. (It is important to label actions that are violations of human rights as such.) This lesson will require several days.

FREEDOM LESSON 9

Rights and Responsibilities

Discuss the following Reflection Points, applying them to the context the class has been discussing in the last couple of lessons:

- ♦ There can be full freedom when rights are balanced with responsibilities.
- ♦ There is full freedom when everyone has equal rights.

Freedom

Ask:

- Why is it said that freedom exists when we use our rights in a balanced and responsible way?
- What responsibilities do certain rights bring?

For younger students, concrete examples should be given when introducing this concept. For example, "When we are allowed to have a pet, what responsibilities come with that right?"

FREEDOM LESSON 10
Art and Liberty

One way of understanding what has happened in the world is through the language of the arts—painting, sculpture, poetry, music and dance. Look for examples in the different cultures of the students or in the curriculum. Depending on the age of the students, they can be exposed to the different art forms. Ask them to write stories or essays from the perspective of an artist.

—*Contributed by Sabine Levy*

FREEDOM LESSON 11
From Resolving Conflicts to Creating Solutions

There may be a conflict at school in which students have different ideas or behaviors that do not leave space for the ideas or

Freedom

behaviors of others—at a physical or emotional level. For example, there might be a problem with distribution of space on the playground or distribution of resources for games.

Listen to the needs of others. Then mention the Reflection Point: All people have a right to be free. For all to be free, each one has to respect the rights of others.

Tell the students that you would like them to use their minds not just to resolve the conflict, but to create something better. Hence, you would like them to pause for two minutes and imagine what they want; to imagine the very best solution. Then ask:

- What do you want?
- Is it beneficial for you?
- What was the best solution you could imagine?
- Is it beneficial for others?
- Is it possible?
- Do we all agree?
- What do we need to do to put it into practice?
- What do you need?
- How do you do it?

Generate solutions that meet everyone's needs. This process can be developed with time as the students learn to use their minds in a creative and constructive way. The relevant steps of the process are imagining, sharing, negotiating, accepting and deciding how to carry the plan out practically.

—*Based on a contribution by Pilar Quera Colomina*

Freedom

TWELVE

12. UNITY UNIT

Unity

Unity Reflection Points

♦ Unity is harmony within and among individuals in the group.

♦ Unity continues by accepting and appreciating each person and his or her contribution.

♦ Unity is built from a shared goal, hope or vision.

♦ Unity makes big tasks seem easy.

♦ The greatness of unity is that everyone is respected.

♦ One note of disrespect can cause unity to be broken.

♦ Unity creates the experience of cooperation, increases enthusiasm for the task and makes the atmosphere empowering.

♦ Unity creates a sense of belonging and increases well-being for all.

Unity Unit

GOAL: To enjoy the feeling of unity.

OBJECTIVES:

❏ To enjoy participating in a polyrhythmic unity activity.

❏ To create a group painting while focusing on the feeling of unity—and practicing valuing the work of others and not intruding.

❏ To sing a song with united hand movements or to dance unity.

GOAL: To increase knowledge about unity.

OBJECTIVES:

❏ To participate in discussions about the Unity Reflection Points and be able to talk about two or more.

❏ To learn about animals which demonstrate unity.

❏ To study one type of animal which demonstrates unity and prepare "advice" from that animal for humankind.

❏ To choose three elements they think are most important to unity.

GOAL: To learn about the need for unity in relation to the world.

OBJECTIVES:

❏ To create a shared goal, hope or vision as a group, and to make part of that real through making and carrying out a plan of action.

❏ To adapt and improve, as needed, the Good Communication Rules developed during the unit on cooperation while working on the class unity project.

❏ To discuss qualities needed to improve the world, and to create a united hands display or write a piece of contrast poetry.

❏ To discuss the problems and needs of the world and assign them an order. For each group of students to make a presentation about how groups could unite in order to solve the problems.

Unity Lessons

Add to the above list of Reflection Points using favorite sayings from your culture, from legends or quotes from respected individuals.

Continue to play a song daily.

Do one of the Relaxation/Focusing exercises every day or every several days, as suitable for your class. The students may enjoy making up their own.

Unity

UNITY LESSON 1

Polyrhythmic Unity

Discuss what unity means, and consider the following Reflection Points:

♦ Unity is harmony within and among individuals in the group.
♦ Unity is built from a shared goal, hope or vision.

Give an example of unity: Bands and orchestras are examples of unity. The musicians have a common goal of playing a particular song. Each one uses his or her talent to achieve the goal by playing his or her individual part well. The guitar or bass creates one type of sound, the drums another, the piano or keyboard another. Ask, "How would an orchestra or band sound if there were lack of unity? How do we sound when there is lack of unity here?" Invite the students to try the following exercise in unity.

Polyrhythmic Unity

This rhythmic clapping exercise is from the Congo. Simpler than it looks, it can be done with participants sitting or standing. Divide the class into four groups.

Group One is to keep the basic rhythm by clapping the numbered beats:

	1	2	3	4
Group Two will clap:	1	pause	3	pause
Group Three will clap:	1	2	pause	4
Group Four will clap:	1	pause	3	4

It can be done without explanation. Having indicated which is Group One, simply get them clapping 1 2 3 4. Then move on to Group Two, and get them clapping 1 _ 3 _. Group One may try to follow you; just go back to them and clap 1 2 3 4, then go to Group Two and clap 1 _ 3 _. Keep doing this until both groups are clear about what they are to do.

Then start Group Three with 1 2 _ 4, moving back to Group Two and One with their own rhythms. Then go on to Group Four with their clap of 1 _ 3 4. Go back to the other groups if necessary.

If anyone is losing the rhythm, just bring them back to it. When everyone is settled into their group's rhythm, ask them to listen to the music they have just created—and then gradually encourage them to clap more quietly so that the sound just gently fades away.

—Contributed by Diana Beaver

UNITY LESSON 2

Learning from Nature

Lesson 2

Tell or read stories about the animals that demonstrate unity, such as geese, dolphins and elephants. There are many true stories about dolphins saving humans. In one, a group of dolphins swam many miles, pushing a man on a raft who was lost at sea. The dolphins took turns pushing the raft with their noses. They were united in their goal of saving the man. When some of the dolphins were tired, others would take over. They kept swimming together, and when others were tired, the ones

Unity

who were more rested would push again. They rotated for many, many miles, pushing the raft until it was close to a little village by the sea, where the man could swim safely by himself to the shore.

Elephants have many similarities to humans. They live for seventy to eighty years. They love their children very much. When the elephants live in a jungle and are threatened by a tiger or lion, the large elephants form a circle around the baby and young elephants. The parent elephants face outward in the circle so that they can guard their children and keep them safe. If a tiger comes, they grab it with their trunk and toss it. The elephants are united; they act together with a shared goal.

Activity

Divide the class into several groups. Ask each group to study an animal known for its support of its kind, and discuss the following Reflection Points in regard to the animal studied.

♦ Unity creates a sense of belonging and increases well-being for all.
♦ The greatness of unity is that everyone is respected.

After their study, groups can discuss what lessons their animal has for humankind. Groups are to artistically prepare their "advice" when presenting their findings to the rest of the class.

UNITY LESSON 3

Painting Unity

Discuss

- What is unity?
- Is part of unity respecting others, valuing other's work, helping but not intruding? How do we do that?

Activity

Provide music, colorful paints, brushes and a long piece of background paper. Ask them to simply create something in silence, just listening to the music and focusing on the feeling of unity. With older groups, stop the music occasionally as a signal for them to move to the right or left.

Share the experience after the students have painted. Discuss the following Reflection Points in relation to the experience:

- ◆ Unity continues by accepting and appreciating each person and his or her contribution.
- ◆ One note of disrespect can cause unity to be broken.

—Contributed by Linda Heppenstall

UNITY LESSON 4

Story—"A Team United"

Read "A Team United" in the Appendix.

Unity

Discuss the story in relation to the Reflection Points the students feel are most relevant. Ask the students what elements they think are most important in creating unity. Ask them to pick the three elements they feel are most important and share why within a small group.

Lesson 5

UNITY LESSON 5

Classroom Unity

Discuss

As a group, decide on a shared goal, hope or vision which all students feel would make something closer to the way they want it to be. Discuss how that vision or goal can take practical form. Make an action plan. It could be a non-physical plan, such as all students deciding they want to do their best—and a practical method for achieving that would be to encourage each other. Perhaps the class has noticed that a particular group is ostracizing some children on the playground. While the adults have talked to them, subtle discrimination occurs which the adults cannot see. The class could decide to speak up for the children being discriminated against, using friendly methods. "Yeah, Tom, we're rainbow friendly around here." The class could decide to spread harmony in the world. Students could decide to do this not only at school but also at home by playing for thirty minutes a day with their younger brothers and sisters. Each day, discuss what is working and what is difficult.

Note: The concept of unity often creates a sense of belonging. In

carrying out a project, it is important to increase that sense within
the group without ostracizing those who may not be involved.

Students may want to become unified in creating something
physical. They may wish to plan a party for someone special,
plant a vegetable garden or paint a mural for the school.
Whatever you plan, enjoy doing it as you create.

Occasionally look at the process, and ask the students to
assess what creates and what detracts from the feeling of unity.
Perhaps they can add to or adapt their Good Communication
Rules from the Cooperation Unit.

Discuss the following Reflection Points:

♦ Unity creates the experience of cooperation, increases enthusiasm for the task and makes the atmosphere empowering.
♦ Unity makes big tasks seem easy.

UNITY LESSON 6

United Hands

Lesson

6

Discuss

On a day after the class has decided on its project, ask students what qualities they think are needed to carry it out. Note
that the qualities people feel they need are often different for different people. Then ask:

• What qualities do you need to improve the world?
• Are the qualities the same or different from the ones you
need to carry out our project?

Unity

Eight to Eleven Activity: Provide a variety of colored paper from which the students can choose. Instruct them to make an outline of their hands. After it is cut out, write on each finger an important quality for the project. All the cutouts can be joined across a wall under the title: "We, the students, united to improve the world."

Twelve to Fourteen Activity: Tell the students they may write their qualities on the hands, or they may want to write a sentence that inspires them on each palm. Perhaps a small group would like to make a picture of the project being accomplished. That could be placed at the top of a board with the hand cutouts supporting it underneath.

—Contributed by Marcia Maria Lins de Medeiros

Alternate Eleven to Fourteen Activity: Contrast Poetry. Ask students to brainstorm vocabulary associated with unity and disunity. They can use a dictionary and thesaurus to find synonyms and antonyms. As a group or as individuals, students can write poetry to take the reader from one feeling or idea to its opposite.

—Contributed by Ruth Liddle

Lesson 7

UNITY LESSON 7

A Play

An ancient tale of a father and his three sons is retold in the form of a play below. The father is concerned as he is getting older that his sons are not taking good care of the land. They quarrel about how to do things when they are together. The father wanted them to learn to be united. So he tied a large

Unity

bundle of thick sticks together with a rope, and then he asked each of his sons, one by one, to break the bundle of sticks. When none of them succeeded, he removed the rope and gave a few sticks to each of his sons to break. The lesson is that there is strength in unity.

Activity

The students may enjoy doing the following play. Or perhaps they would like to make up one of their own.

Scene One

Setting: The King is sitting on his throne thinking deeply. His face looks concerned. A guard is standing at the other end of the room. The Minister enters the throne room.

Minister: "What's the problem, your Majesty? You look so concerned and unhappy."

King: "Yes, my Minister, I am unhappy. My three sons are busy traveling and hunting and having fun without being concerned about anything else. And when I ask them to help manage the land and deal with the guards, they only quarrel."

Suddenly, the king sits up straighter and says to the Minister: "I want you to bring to me a bundle of thick sticks tied with a strong rope."

The King then turns to the guard standing at the door of the hall and says to him: "Go and call my children to come and join me now."

Scene Two

The King is sitting on his throne. The Minister is standing at his side. In front of him are his sons. In between the King and his sons is a bundle of sticks, tied with a rope.

King: "My sons, I want you to try to break this bundle of sticks in half."

The youngest son: "I can do it. I'm very strong."

But, try as he might, the youngest son is not able to break the bundle of sticks. Each one of them tries and fails.

The King: "Minister, loosen the rope." (To his sons): "None of you, by yourselves, could break that bundle of sticks. How can this task be done? (pause) Unwrap the bundle. I want each one of you to take one-third of the sticks and try to break them."

The sons do as they are instructed. The King looks at his sons.

King: "Did you notice that you could not break the sticks when you tried to do so alone? When you worked together, you accomplished the task easily. This is what I want from you—to always work together. When you are united, you are strong, and you will solve each problem easily."

—*Contributed by Lamia El-Dajani*

Activity

Divide the students into groups and ask them to think about what the world needs. Tell them you want them to think of the problems of the world as being a bundle of one hundred sticks. The people of the world can solve the problems if they unite. What are the problems and needs of the world, and how many sticks is each problem? (For example, world hunger may get

Unity

eight sticks out of the hundred.) Ask each group of students to discuss this and decide what groups of people could develop unity to solve each problem. Each group is to make a presentation. They may illustrate their oral presentation with artistic representations or with graphs.

The educator may wish to instruct older students to apply their information about corporations or international institutions. They may wish to share their information with those corporations and institutions.

UNITY LESSON 8

Artistic Expression

For the school's next International Day, Peace Day or Values Day (you set the date), plan to do a skit you have done in the classroom, and present some of your slogans and ideas. Also, prepare several songs and dances about unity. Develop hand movements to correspond with one song so all hands move in unison. Circle folk dances and line dances are fun and can be an excellent display of unity.

Values Fair

A Values Fair was proposed by Marcia Lins de Medeiros from Brazil. It is a great idea for the school's next celebration, party or play day. Several classes can provide the materials for a game or two to create an array of activities.

The teachers and students can discuss, explore and learn about values as they prepare the materials for the games. Preparation may take a couple of weeks. Enjoy the process, for that is what is important. Actively include the students in discussing and deciding what they want to do. Positively reinforce the students for using values-based skills and cooperative behaviors as they work on the activities. Occasionally stop the activity to debrief behaviors contributing to unity or taking away from unity. While this has been done with students eight to eleven years old, you may find the twelve- to fourteen-year-old students are interested. Ask them and see. Make up your own games, or try a variety of the following:

Lucky Fishing
Preparatory Activities

Make fish out of cardboard or paper. Students can decorate one side as a fish and write positive messages or definitions of values on the other side. Ask the students to create their own messages. They may wish to have different colors for the different values messages written on the back of the fish. During the preparation time, the teacher can work with the students on choosing messages that feel good or which motivate them. They can experiment with this by writing their messages, putting them in a box and picking one daily.

Create slogans for your booth, such as "Pick your quality of the day" or "Catch a message."

Prepare the booth and "fishing poles."

Game:

Students can use "fishing poles" made of cardboard and string and drop their "line" behind a large sheet of paper with water drawn on it. Other students hidden by the large sheet of paper could attach the "values fish" to the line. Or students could toss a ping-pong ball at openings or small bowls and receive the paper fish inside the opening or bowl.

Bowling Down Negativities

Preparatory Activities

Discuss the negative feelings and habits that create loss of hope or self-doubt, or which interfere in relationships with others. Ask: "What negative feelings would you like to conquer?"

Students can collect used plastic bottles (such as drink containers) and decorate them with paint or cut-out paper, then put sand in the bottom for weight. Each student can label a bottle with a negative quality, such as fear, laziness, anger, stubbornness, disrespect, impatience, etc.

Game:

Line up a few bottles in a close "V" shape, similar to the shape of pins at a bowling alley. Ask the student which positive quality they are going to use to knock down the negativities. Ask them to write that quality on a piece of paper that is pasted to the ball. (Two balls should be available.) One student at a time can roll a ball toward the pins, aiming to knock them all down. Assure a greater degree of success for young students by having a sufficiently large ball and only a little bit of sand in the bottles.

Unity

A basketball could be used with larger drink containers. Vary the distance according to the age and coordination of the students. Give encouragement and cheer their success.

Values Egg and Spoon Race
Preparation:

Discuss with the students what qualities they think are important to create a better world. The students can each paint a values egg. (While it is good if some values are repeated, make sure there are eggs for each value they feel is important.)

Make a picture of a world for the finish line. A picture four feet in diameter would be excellent, as then the students can sit or stand around it and have their picture taken at the end of the race.

Game:

In the "values egg and spoon race" students decide which value they think is important for a better world, paint that value on their egg and then line up with other participants at the starting line. A picture of the world or a globe could be at the finish line. Once the racers reach the finish line, they may place their values egg on the world.

Option: If not enough eggs are available, they could race in pairs. Pairs paint the egg together and then race together, one holding the egg and spoon and both holding on to a ribbon which they must not let go of. The pairs race would require a little more cooperation by students, as each pair would have to agree which value they think is most important for a better world and they would have to take great care of the egg.

Values Roulette
Preparation:

Make a roulette wheel. Instead of numbers, put the names of the twelve values on the roulette wheel. Write them in the pie-wedged shapes of the circle. (If the students have developed Reflection Points for other values, include those values as well.)

Game:

The student playing the game calls out the value he or she wants the needle or ball to land on. He or she wins a prize if it lands on the value—and if the student can give a Reflection Point for that value. The student may opt for another turn to win a prize if a Reflection Point is given for the value on which the needle or ball lands.

Bingo
Preparation:

Make beautiful bingo cards with the names of qualities and values in the squares, and put the names of all those qualities and values on separate small pieces of paper. Provide beans as markers and a few prizes for the winners.

The class will need to have lots of qualities in order to have a variety of cards. They may wish to add to the following list: attention, balance, benevolence, caring, cheerfulness, clarity, cleanliness, constancy, contentment, cooperation, courage, determination, discipline, eagerness, enthusiasm, flexibility, friendliness, generosity, gentleness, goodwill, happiness, honesty, humility, humor, initiative, integrity, kindness, lightness, loving, mercy, patience, peace, self-confidence, self-respect, serenity, simplicity, smartness, stability, sweetness, tolerance, truth and wisdom.

Game:

Play bingo, with the leader picking out the name of a quality on a slip of paper and calling it out as students put a bean on the quality that was called on their card (five squares by five squares with the middle square being "free"). Give a prize to the first one who has beans on five squares in a row (horizontal, vertical or diagonal).

Dove Game

Do the Dove Game in the Peace Unit, making a large game board on the lawn.

Dances

Enjoy circle dances from different cultures, or let the students choose dances they did during other values units and would like to do again. For example, some may wish to do a cooperation dance or a freedom dance.

Face Painting

Face painting is popular with many students. Older students can use acrylic paints to paint the symbol the students wish—perhaps a peace star, heart, rainbow, etc.

Food

Make cakes in heart or dove shapes, or provide food from different cultures of the world.

Unity

APPENDIX

Item 1: Peace

Example of a World Cake

By a Student in China

Angel World Cake

Dry

2½ cups Happiness—scatter evenly

1¾ cups Freedom—distribute equally

1½ cups Trust—grate and toss in bowl

1 pinch Laughter—sift throughout mixture

a dash of Helpful People—radiating out from center

Wet

2 cups Respect—pour and mix well

1½ cups Cleanliness—spread on bottom of pan

1 cup Understanding—mix throughout batter

¼ cup Friendship—mix until doughy

Toppings

1½ cups Peace—spread on finished cake

1 tbsp. Unity—sprinkle on top

1 tsp. Love—sprinkle lightly everywhere

Steps

1. Spread cleanliness on bottom of circular pan with a circumference of the equator.
2. Mix friendship, respect and understanding in a bowl. Allow to sit for one minute.
3. Mix trust, helpful people, happiness, freedom and laughter into a separate bowl. Beat for one minute.
4. Mix ingredients together in one bowl. Blend for two minutes.

Item 2: All Values

Mind Maps

A Mind Map is a powerful graphic technique that engages both sides of the brain through utilizing words, images, numbers, logic, rhythm, color, imagination and spatial awareness. It can be used in many different ways—to outline stories, plan talks, organize details for functions, or to create and develop thoughts about a topic. It is simple to use. In fact, using the values words is an excellent way to begin to learn Mind Mapping. Place a value word in the middle of a page placed horizontally, draw some lines extending outward, and simply place on each line one word which immediately pops into your mind when you think of that word. Your brain will automatically use its power of association.

In *Get Ahead* by Vanda North and Tony Buzan, they suggest using Mind Mapping when brainstorming a topic, a technique they named "Brain Bloom." As the authors say, "It allows a great blossoming, flowering, associating, connecting and flowering of your thoughts, ideas and facts, captured in their radiant beauty." Rules for Mind Mapping are outlined below.

How to Mind Map

1. Take a blank piece of paper and place it horizontally.

2. Start in the center with a Central Image that personally represents the topic about which you are writing/thinking. Use at least three colors in the image.

3. The Main Themes around the Central Image are like the chapter headings of a book. Print the words and place them on lines of the same length. The central lines can be curved and organic, i.e., like branches of a tree to the trunk.

4. Start to add a Second Level of thought. These words or images are linked to the main branch that triggered them. The lines connect and are thinner.

5. Add a Third or Fourth Level of data, as thoughts come to you. Use images as much as you can. Allow your thoughts to come freely, meaning you "hop about" the Mind Map as the links and associations occur to you.

6. Add Dimension to your Mind Maps. Box and add depth around the word or image, use different colors and styles, and if you like, add arrows to show connections.

7. Have fun making each Mind Map a little more beautiful, artistic, colorful and imaginative. Develop your own personal style.

Item 3: Peace

Conflict Resolution Steps

Ask both students: Do you want help? Are you willing to work on a solution?

If both answer "yes," proceed. If one says "no," tell them both to go to the office.

To Student One:
What's your name?

To Student One:
Please tell us what happened.

To Student Two:
Please tell us what happened.

To Student One:
How did you feel when that happened?

To Student Two:
How did you feel when that happened?

To Student One:
What would you like to stop?

To Student Two:
What would you like to stop?

To Student One:
What would you like him or her to do instead?

To Student One:
What would you like him or her to do instead?

To Student One:
Can you do that?

To Student Two:
What's your name?

To Student Two:
Please repeat what he or she said.

To Student One:
Please repeat what he or she said.

To Student Two:
Please repeat what he or she said.

To Student One:
Please repeat what he or she said.

To Student Two:
Please repeat what he or she said.

To Student One:
Please repeat what he or she said.

To Student Two:
Please repeat what he or she said.

To Student Two:
Please repeat what he or she said.

To Student Two:
Can you do that?

To both: Can you make a firm commitment to try to behave in the way you both have agreed? If they both say "yes," compliment their good listening and working on a solution.

If one of them says "no," ask each student to think of something he or she would like the two to do that would solve the problem. Ask them to think of ideas until they both agree they have a good solution and can commit to trying to carry it through.

Item 4: Peace

Cool Off

A Peace Rap Song by Max and Marcia Nass

Cool off, cool off, cool off, cool off!
Solving problems is hard when you're mad,
Walk away, cool off, you'll be glad.
(Repeat)

When you're angry at someone, it's not easy to have fun,
You'll get madder if you stay. Get smart and just walk away.

You don't need to start a fight to prove who's wrong and who is right.
Remember the good times you had, and then you won't feel so bad.

Take deep breaths and cool off. Find a friend to listen to you talk.
You just want peace, my friend, to make your anger end.

Cool off, cool off, cool off, cool off!
Solving problems is hard when you're mad,
Walk away, cool off, you'll be glad.

Mind your own business. Don't make threats.
Play with people who don't fight.
Don't call names, just be kind. Everything will be all right.

When you're angry at someone, it's not easy to have fun.
You'll get madder if you stay. Get smart and just walk away.

You don't need to start a fight to prove who's wrong and who is right.
Remember the good times you had, and then you won't feel so bad.

Take deep breaths and cool off. Find a friend to listen to you talk.
You just want peace, my friend, to make your anger end.

Cool off, cool off, cool off, cool off!
Solving problems is hard when you're mad,
Walk away, cool off, you'll be glad.

Item 5: Respect

Lily the Leopard

By John McConnel

Lily the Leopard thought there was something gravely wrong with her. Unlike all the other leopards she knew, her spots were not black but pink. It would not have been so terrible if the other leopards had accepted her. But the other leopards would not accept her. In fact, even her own family shunned her. Her mother had cried upon seeing her baby daughter covered in pink spots, and her father and her two brothers, Julian and Ricky, were ashamed to have such a strange-looking leopard in the family. The other leopards in the neighborhood ignored her, laughed at her and sometimes poked at her, just because her spots were a different color from their spots. Sometimes she felt afraid and sad, and other times she got very angry. So she decided that she would stay alone most of the time. She spent her days lying in a bush, watching the other leopards frolic about. Even when they would occasionally call Lily to come out to play, she would remember their past insults and would growl low in response to their invitation.

It was not her fault she had pink spots! She was different and could not help it. Often she wondered why the other leopards didn't understand. She had done her best to rid herself of her pink spots. Lily tried scrubbing and washing them away. She tried bleaching them. Once she even painted them black, but the pink soon shone through the paint. Nothing worked. After a while, she realized that she was stuck with them. What else could she do?

One day, after four young cubs were teasing her, Lily decided to run away from home. She had had enough. She ran off into the jungle as fast as she could. Lily ran for hours, just stopping to rest now and then and to wipe the tears from her eyes.

Eventually, she came to rest in a clearing and fell asleep. She was awakened by the soft touch of a tongue on her nose. As she looked up, she saw the most amazing sight. Before her stood a great big leopard with bright green spots! Lily was so surprised by what she saw that she blinked twice just to make sure she wasn't dreaming. She had often had dreams of other leopards with different colored spots, but she never imagined that there actually were such leopards. The great leopard with bright green spots told her his name was Lenny and asked her what she was doing so far from home. As he spoke, he seemed to glow with confidence and happiness. His eyes were filled with kindness, and so Lily felt safe and soon found herself telling her story.

Lenny quietly listened to her story. When she finished, he gave her a warm hug and helped her dry her eyes. He then smiled at her and said, "What you need is some self-respect."

"I do?" asked Lily. "What's that?"

"Self-respect means liking yourself, even when others do not," said Lenny. "It means appreciating all the special things about yourself."

"There's nothing special about me, except these pink spots and I hate them!" she cried. "I am so strange and ugly. I wish I was never born!"

"Don't be silly," said Lenny. "You're very special. There is no one like you in the whole world, and I can see that you have many good qualities." Lenny paused for a moment. He seemed to be thinking. "I have an idea," he said. "Let's make a list of all the things you like about yourself."

"Okay," said Lily, brightening a little. She sat for a few moments thinking and then said: "Well, I'm kind and caring, and I try to be friendly. I help my mom and dad and I'm very loving . . ." Lily paused for a moment, her voice trailing off. Lenny nodded his head eagerly in order to encourage her. Lily felt safe again and so she continued. "I have beautiful gold eyes, and I'm a very fast runner. I'm brave and strong and . . ."

Just then Lucy the Leopard appeared with Laura the Leopard. Lucy was covered with blue spots and Laura in purple spots. As soon as they saw Lily, they were delighted. They smiled grandly and leaped into the air. "What a lovely leopard you are, and what a beautiful coat you have!"

"Thank you," Lily replied, smiling as she remembered there was much more to her than met the eye. Suddenly, she felt much better.

"It's okay to be different," she thought. "In fact, I think my spots are rather pretty! If other leopards do not like me because of my pink spots, that's because they don't know better. I'm okay. I'm glad I'm unique."

Lily spent a few more hours playing with her newly found and brightly colored friends. But as the sun began to set, Lily began to think about her family. They might be worried about her, she thought. Lily waved good-bye to Lenny and Lucy and Laura. She promised them, however, that she would visit them again soon and off she went. As she walked home, she watched the sun set. For the first time, she noticed the many brilliant colors in the sky. The sky was pink, blue, green, purple and orange. "How beautiful," she thought. "I wonder why I never noticed all those colors before."

When Lily finally arrived home, her mom and dad and two brothers ran to meet her. As they came closer to Lily, they noticed there was something different about her. She seemed to shimmer and glow. She held her head high as she trotted forward and smiled at them warmly. "She is really quite beautiful," they thought. And they wondered why they had never noticed that before.

Item 6: Respect

The Two Birds

By H. Otero, from *Parabolas en son de paz*

Two birds were very happy in the same tree, a willow tree. One of them rested on a branch at the highest part of the willow; the other one was down below, where one branch joined another.

After a while, the bird perched in the highest part of the tree said, to break the ice, "Oh, what beautiful green leaves these are!"

The bird resting on the branch below took this statement as a provocation. He replied in a curt manner, "Are you blind? Can't you see they are white?"

The one in the highest part, upset, answered, "It's you who is blind! They are green!"

The other bird, from below with his beak pointed upward, responded, "I bet my tail feathers they are white. You don't know anything."

The bird at the top felt his temper flare up and, without thinking twice, he jumped down to the same branch as his adversary to teach him a lesson.

The other bird did not move. The two birds were so close, they stood eye to eye. Their feathers were ruffled with rage. In their tradition, they both looked above before they started the fight.

The bird that had come down from above said with much surprise, "How strange! Look at the leaves, they are white!" And he invited his friend, "Come up to where I was before."

They flew to the highest branch of the willow tree, and this time they said together, "Look at the leaves, they are so green!"

Item 7: Respect

Fire in the Jungle

By Henny Trailes

A gigantic fire broke out in the jungle. The animals flocked together on the other side of the lake, and they gazed at the flames. A small bird, seeing what was going on, took a drop of water in its little beak and let it drop on the flames. It returned, took another little drop in its beak and let it fall. And like this it flew back and forth diligently.

The rest of the animals just watched him and said to each other: "And does this one think he can actually do something with his little drop of water?" At one stage they asked him, "Tell us, little bird, do you honestly believe you can put out the fire with your little drop of water?"

The little bird answered: "I do what I must." Just then, an angel went by, saw the little bird and produced a great rainfall. The fire went out.

Henny Trailes is an actress in Argentina. Used with permission from Visions of a Better World.

Item 8: Peace and Respect

Situation Cards

SITUATION CARD ONE

Situation: Another student in your class borrowed your favorite pencil (or pen) last week and has not returned it. You have not seen him or her using it today in class.

Questions: How do you feel?

What can you do?

If you decide to talk with him or her, what would you say?

SITUATION CARD TWO

Situation: Two of your best friends are really angry with each other. They are not talking to each other now, but both of them are talking with you.

Questions: How do you feel?

What can you do? What might help?

If you decide to talk with them, what would you say?

SITUATION CARD THREE

Situation: Another student at school is picking on you and seems to be trying to get you to fight with him or her.

Questions: How do you feel?
How could you respond using the value of peace?
How could you respond using the value of respect?
Act out your responses.

SITUATION CARD FOUR

Situation: Your best friend's mother has just died.

Questions: How do you think your friend feels?
What can you do to help her or him?

SITUATION CARD FIVE

Situation: A country near your own has just fired missiles at another country. It looks as if a war will start.

Questions: How do you feel?

What would you like to tell the leaders of both of those countries?

What do you think they should do?

How can you respond to the situation using the values of peace and respect?

SITUATION CARD SIX

Situation: It's your first day at a new school. You are opening the door to enter your new classroom for the first time.

Questions: How do you feel?

How would you like the other students to treat you?

SITUATION CARD SEVEN

Situation: You've just failed an important exam.

Questions: How do you feel?

Are you still a good person? (There is a "right" answer to this question: YES, you still are a good person.)

How would you have liked to do on the exam?

What can you do next time to do better?

What kinds of things do you say (to yourself) that discourage you?

What kinds of things can you say (to yourself) to encourage yourself?

SITUATION CARD EIGHT

Situation: There is a student in your class who sometimes criticizes you. He or she has just criticized you again.

Questions: How do you feel?

What value do you need?

What thoughts can you say (to yourself) that will help you stay in self-respect?

What could you say to the criticizing person while staying in self-respect?

Act it out.

Item 9: Love

The Four Thrones

By Wendy Marshall

Once upon a time there were four benevolent sovereigns who ruled the Earth. Each had great respect for the other, and the world was in harmony. At a sacred place of four thrones, the four rulers would meet to exchange news of their kingdoms.

But a time came when their people became bored with noble qualities. They wanted the thrill of winners and losers, the contrast of rich and poor.

The four sovereigns decided to leave their kingdoms and let their people rule themselves. They all agreed to silently wander the Earth and return as sovereigns only when their people wanted to live in peace again.

Many years later, when the Earth and its people had become spoiled by greed, ego and selfishness, a young girl read the story of the four sovereigns. She realized this was not a fairy tale. She vowed that when she grew up, she would search for the four sovereigns and ask them to return to their kingdoms so that harmony could prevail once again.

After many years of searching, she reached the high mountain foretold. There she found the four thrones that faced outward to the valley below. She waited there, since in the legend it was said that each year the sovereigns came to the place where the four thrones faced outward over the valley to meet and give news of their lands. Months passed.

One day, an old traveler came by and asked the young woman about her quest. The traveler listened intently. She then told her that the sovereigns would only meet her when she had learned to look within and let peace grow in her heart. They would meet her when her eyes radiated love, when her words were guided by wisdom and when her actions brought only happiness to others.

The traveler agreed to teach the young woman these lost arts, and the young woman studied diligently. On the day she was ready, the old traveler took her leave. At sunrise the next morning, four figures approached. Queen Wisdom took her place on one throne, and King Love, Queen Peace and King Happiness all assumed their thrones. The young woman entered the circle and told them of her quest.

As Queen Wisdom addressed her, she recognized that this was her teacher, the old traveler. "Go back to your land and teach all who come to you the things you have been taught here. You are the seed that will bear the fruit of harmony throughout the earth once again. Keep courage. There will be many tests. But the seed of hope will soon grow, and when all hearts are ready, we will return.

"Remember, all human hearts contain beautiful qualities. Don't be fooled by bitterness and hatred. These treasures you have found within yourself will touch others deeply. Never stop believing in yourself and the task will be accomplished quickly."

Item 10: Tolerance

The Shorties and the Tallies

Based on a Story by John McConnel

There was once a land where all the people were either short and fat or tall and thin. There was no one in between. The "Shorties" and "Tallies," as they were called, did not like each other. Each thought himself to be better than the other. When the Shorties were talking among themselves about the arrogance of the Tallies, they would call them "beanpoles." The Tallies would talk to each other about how stupid the "shrimps" were. The "beanpoles" and "shrimps" were always arguing and fighting, and there was no peace in the land.

The Shorties and the Tallies did not know each other very well. They never tried to be friends. Indeed, they both refused to have anything to do with the other. They refused to live next door to one another, used different shops, and their children even went to different schools. Separate businesses and even churches and temples were built to meet the needs of the Shorties and Tallies. Demand grew for the land to be divided in two, and there was talk of war as the "beanpoles" blamed the "shrimps" for problems in the land. Each side rushed to buy guns. The ruler of the land did not help. Most of the time he was interested in accumulating more wealth for himself. Sometimes he even blamed the Tallies for the problems of the land. As intolerance increased, even the children were told by adults that the other group was not good. The children of the Shorties were told to not make friends with the "beanpoles," and the children of the Tallies were told not to make friends with the "shrimps."

Then one day a strange thing happened. All the people of the land went blind. Not even one person could see anything. Everyone's world was turned upside down in more ways than one. The people stumbled around, trying to find their way from the shops and the churches and temples. They were bumping into one another and tripping over each other. Little children, teenagers and adults all needed help, and they helped each other. Adults conversed with anyone they bumped into to ask for help in finding their way. Little children were taken care of by older children, and mothers of both Shorties and Tallies helped each other find their children.

At first, the Shorties did not know they were sometimes being helped by "beanpoles," and Tallies did not realize they were being helped by "shrimps." They welcomed the understanding voices and the generous help. But as they helped each other with their hands, they began to realize that some of those kind hands were thin and long, and other kind hands were short and plump.

"Hmmph," one Shortie named Miriam said to herself, "I bet that's the only nice beanpole out there." But as Miriam tried to find her way to the store to buy food, she was again helped by another Tallie!

Ali, one of the Tallies, was also surprised. "Those shrimps aren't all so mean," he thought to himself one day when a Shortie helped him find his little brother.

As one long week and another week passed, each person began to realize that the shape and size of each other's bodies no longer mattered. They began to judge each person they met by his or her behavior instead of appearance—whether they were kind and gentle or mean-spirited. They began to appreciate their new friends and understand that a person's character is much more important than the way he or she looks—and that good qualities can be found in everyone.

With this realization, the hearts of the short, fat people and the tall, thin people began to melt. They were kinder to everyone they met. As they began to grow fond of their new friends, their sight returned just as suddenly as it had disappeared! They laughed with each other in their joy of seeing, and they promised never to be deceived by their eyes again.

Item 11: Happiness

The Heart School

By Diana Hsu

Marc lived in a small town not far away from here. He lived with his mother in a small house. The house was surrounded by grassy fields and huge trees, and the school he went to was within walking distance. Marc sometimes thought how lucky he was not to have to live in one of those large cities, where there were hardly any parks in which he could play with his friends.

Besides playing outside a lot, Marc liked to spend time in his room. He was always busy. He liked to collect stamps from all over the world, play with his cars and buses, Lego toys and airplanes. But one thing he did not like very much was going to school.

One Monday morning, as he started to walk to school, he somehow felt this would be a very special day. It was a bright day, the sun was shining, the birds were singing, beautiful butterflies were flying by and the air was filled with the sweet fragrance of colorful flowers. He felt as if this would really be the most special day in his whole life. Marc stopped walking. He lay down on the grass and closed his eyes. As he started to enjoy this, he relaxed. Then suddenly, with his eyes still closed, he saw himself walking ahead and reaching a heart-shaped house. As he came nearer to this house, he could feel that this was a very special place. Now he could read the letters above the door:

The School for Loving Children

As if by a magnet, Marc was drawn to look through the window and . . . "Ooohh!" he exclaimed, ". . . what a wonderful world!" He saw a classroom decorated with light-colored paintings of butterflies, rainbows, flowers and happy children playing. He saw mobiles of angels, stars and hearts. The curtains and furniture were brightly colored, and in the windows were transparent pictures and collages through which the light was shining like a rainbow.

Marc saw the teacher and her children sitting in a circle on a carpet. He looked at the faces of the children. They were sparkling with happiness. And then his eyes were drawn to one particular child. "It's me! It's really me!" he thought. "I am one of these happy, loving children, shining with so much joy!" Marc was surprised that suddenly he felt so light—it was as if his heart was saying, "I am a happy, loving child!" And then suddenly the school disappeared. Marc got up from the grass and with light steps continued onward to school, wishing his own school was like the one he had just seen.

The next morning, Marc could hardly wait to reach that same spot on the grass again. He wanted to see that heart school again. He searched and searched, but the school was nowhere to be found. Was it all a dream? Somehow he knew it was not. He felt a sudden disappointment. "I feel . . . I feel . . . I want to cry!" thought Marc.

"Marc, Marc," he heard someone whisper. He looked up, and floating down from the sky, seated on a giant rainbow-balloon, was a smiling Golden Bear. As the balloon landed, the heart-shaped school appeared behind him.

"Hello," said the Golden Bear. Taking Marc's hand, he whispered gently, "Come and see yourself, Marc." And as he looked through the window, he could see himself standing with the others, in a circle and listening to the teacher.

"Maria, can you please play the flute?" the teacher asked.

When Maria started to play her flute, they all started to dance. What fun they were having! And Marc noticed that no one was pushing, breaking the circle, kicking or being nasty to the others, and no one was left out. The room was filled with magical sounds.

As Marc continued to watch, the children and the teacher were moving from one activity to another without any unkind words being spoken. A little while later, Marc saw himself drawing and sharing his pencils with the others. The teacher, with a smiling face and kind eyes, was going from child to child, listening quietly, while each child was telling her about his or her drawings. After all the drawings were finished, Marc saw the children packing away their things and then decorating the walls. Each child was admiring the work of the others. What harmony there was!

The children then sat in groups at their tables and took out their arithmetic books. Everyone quietly listened to the teacher, who spoke in a clear, soft voice, explaining what needed to be done.

Marc watched as the teacher looked over the shoulder of the boy who looked like him and said, "Well done, Marc! All your sums are correct, and your work is neat."

Marc looked up at the Golden Bear. "How can that be me? I am not good at arithmetic. My work is not neat and the teacher is seldom pleased with me!"

The Golden Bear just smiled and held Marc's hand tightly. "Just watch, just watch!"

When Marc looked up through the window again, he saw himself confidently reading aloud to the class. Much to his surprise, everyone was listening eagerly. "Look at that, I can do it, I can do it!" he said to the Golden Bear. "I can read without feeling scared and stumbling over the words!"

"Of course you can!" said the Golden Bear. He seemed to know Marc well. What a wonder!

Then the children sat down in a circle to have their lunch. As the food was passed around, Marc could see himself waiting patiently. No one was pushing and no one was calling out, "Me first! That's mine! Give that to me! I am not your friend anymore." And no one snatched the food away from anyone else.

Marc saw himself asking his friend, "Would you like a piece of cake?"

"Thank you," replied his friend, and he offered Marc some fruit and nuts.

After lunch, Marc noticed that the children seemed happy helping one another. No one laughed at others' mistakes. Everyone seemed to be friends and happy to see one another succeed!

When it was time to go home, the teacher said, "I look forward to seeing you again tomorrow. As Marc saw himself leaving, the teacher turned and smiled, "Good-bye, Marc."

Marc turned to the Golden Bear and asked, "How can I be like that?"

The Golden Bear just smiled and said, "If, from your heart, you really want to change . . . just wait and see . . . just wait and see! Good-bye, Marc." And off the Golden Bear floated.

STOP READING HERE!

CONTINUE READING HERE TOMORROW.

When it was bedtime, Marc thought about how wonderful it would be to dream of the heart-school again. He closed his eyes and waited, but no heart-school appeared. He waited some more and nothing happened. "Oh well," he thought. "It was nice while it lasted." But then, right in front of him, slowly and gently, the Golden Bear floated down to the foot of his bed, holding onto his rainbow-balloon. Marc gave him a big smile and said, "It's you! I was wondering whether I would ever see you again!"

"Hello!" said the Golden Bear, "I was listening to the thoughts of your heart. You want to be the happy you, the real you. Everyone likes to be loved by all."

"Yes," said Marc slowly, "it's like magic how you seem to know everything!"

"Well," said the Golden Bear, "it is not as difficult as you think. Shall I help you a little? I am going to show you a secret. Look, here are two boxes. Read what is written on them."

HAPPY   UNHAPPY

The Golden Bear took the Unhappy Box and asked, "What do you think is in this box?"

"I don't know," replied Marc, "but it can't be anything good!"

The Golden Bear opened the Unhappy Box and took out four cards.

"What's written on them?" Marc asked the Bear impatiently.

"Guess first!" said the Golden Bear.

"Mm, mm . . . I don't know!" responded Marc.

The Golden Bear looked amazed. "But you do know what makes you unhappy, don't you?"

"Well, yes," Marc started slowly, "when I push or hurt others, or if they push or hurt me, that makes me unhappy."

"That's right!" said the Bear. "Now I will read what is written on the cards: pushing and kicking others, speaking harsh and hurtful words, thinking 'I can't do it'; and being impatient."

"Is that what makes me really unhappy?" asked Marc. "When I hurt others or when I am impatient?"

"Yes, that's right," said the Golden Bear, "and then everyone is unhappy with you as well."

"Please take the cards from the Happy Box now," Marc asked the Bear.

The Bear took four cards from the Happy Box and read them to Marc. "Be patient, say only kind words, help others, and always have good thoughts about yourself and others."

"Is this the secret of being happy?" Marc asked.

"Yes," explained the Bear, "and when you are happy, that is when you are the real you! That is why it is so easy to change. I'll help you!" he added, seeing the look on Marc's face.

"Listen very carefully now," said the Golden Bear. "Tomorrow, when you pack your school bag, open the Happy Box and take out one card. Read the message carefully, and when you're in school, just do what the card says. If you follow it, it will work! I'll see you tomorrow evening to hear how your day went."

And swiftly the Golden Bear lifted off and floated away with his rainbow-balloon, waving and smiling as Marc waved and smiled back.

The next morning, Marc got out of bed early and got ready quickly. This was going to be the first day of happiness at school. When everything was ready, Marc took a card out of his Happy Box. As he was taking the first card, it seemed that he could hear the voice of the Golden Bear. "What have you picked, Marc? Tell me."

Astonished, Marc looked around but could not see the little Bear. "Strange," he thought, but he really had heard his voice. "Tell me what you have picked," Marc heard again.

"Okay, I took a card and it says, 'Do everything with a smile,'" Marc said out loud.

"Oh, that is wonderful," Marc could hear the Bear saying. "It is easy! Tell me, what are you going to do?"

Marc started slowly, "I will . . . I will . . . I will say good morning to everyone with a smile. If someone is unfriendly, I will smile instead of hitting him or saying something mean. If my teacher tells me to write neater, I will smile at her instead of getting upset, and . . ." he finished in a rush, "anyway, I will do everything with a smile today."

"Okay," smiled the Golden Bear, "see you this evening!"

When Marc came home from school that day, he could hardly wait to see the little Bear to share all the news with him. Marc looked around and soon the Bear appeared, floating down on his rainbow-balloon.

"I could see your happy face from afar," the Bear said.

"Yes, Bear, oh, it was a wonderful day! I did everything exactly as I told you this morning and guess what? Not only did I smile," Marc said proudly, "but others started to smile, too, and seemed to get along better with each other."

"Well done!" said the Bear.

"Yes," added Marc. "And Hugo wanted to kick me. But I just stood there fearlessly and smiled . . . and you know what happened then? He forgot about kicking me! He sort of looked at me in a funny way and turned around and walked away. I think he forgot about kicking altogether today. It is amazing!" exclaimed Marc. "Oh, I am looking forward to taking another card from the Happy Box tomorrow. Will you come tomorrow to hear about my happy day?"

"Yes, I will come! Good luck for tomorrow, and be strong!" said the Bear. As the Golden Bear was flying off with his balloon, Marc ended the day happily. Oh, how exciting life can be when you discover something new!

The next morning, Marc got up early again and picked his card for the day from the Happy Box. "Little Bear, can you hear me? Today I've picked, be patient. I've thought about what I will do. Shall I tell you?"

"I will let others go first; I will not rush to finish my work too quickly.

(I always want to finish first, so that I get praised.)

I will help others patiently and will wait happily when others are speaking.

I will listen carefully to what my teacher is telling me."

"Oh, I can hardly wait to get to school today!" said Marc.

Marc had a long day at school. His face was not so happy when he got home. He finished his dinner slowly and went to bed early.

"Oh, I almost forgot, the little Golden Bear wanted to come," thought Marc. It was as if the Bear heard his thoughts, for he was suddenly standing right in front of him.

"It wasn't so easy today, was it?" gently asked the Bear, looking at Marc's face.

"Well, do you know what happened? I did everything as I said this morning, but I forgot one thing, and that was to be patient with myself," said Marc. "I rushed to finish quickly, and because of that, I dropped some paint and it splashed all over the floor! And only then did I remember that I wanted to be patient with myself. Bear, it wasn't pleasant at all! You know why? Not only did I drop the paint, but when one of my classmates started to laugh at me and made fun of me, I said some hurtful words to him. And then I felt awful afterwards."

"Cheer up, Marc! You've only just started to become the happier you! That needs a little time, and these things happen sometimes. Just try not to make the same mistake again," the Bear said in his most encouraging manner.

"I'm glad to hear that, Bear. It makes me feel a lot better," said Marc.

With a big smile the Bear opened the Unhappy Box and turned to Marc, saying, "Write down your unhappiness about the spilled paint and about being angry with your classmate, and slip it into the Unhappy Box. Then close the box, and it is over and done with! As easy as that! What's past is past. There's no need to worry or to be upset about it. Try to understand what went wrong, tell yourself that you won't make the same mistake again, and then forget it completely. Remember only what went right today and what made you happy, and think about what you are going to do tomorrow to be happy." The Golden Bear paused a moment, and then he added, "Tomorrow you will try again and you will succeed, and that's a promise! You are loving and very special, Marc!"

Marc suddenly felt so light and full of confidence. "Yes, tomorrow I will try again and succeed! Oh, I can hardly wait until tomorrow to take the next card!" Marc laughed happily as the Bear grabbed the string of his rainbow-balloon and got ready to float away. The Bear looked at him. His eyes were full of love and hope. Suddenly Marc felt that his heart, too, was filling with love and hope. He could feel the great confidence the Bear had in him. "He believes in me and I know it will work! With the help of the little Bear I will be victorious and become the real me, happy and loving!"

Children, now that you have just listened to this story, how do you think it will end? Share your ideas with others in your class or with your family.

Okay, listen now to what happened. Day by day, Marc would take a card from his Happy Box and think about how to use it at school. Most of the time he was good and successful, but sometimes he would make a mistake. When he made a mistake, he would not get upset or worry. Instead, he would try to understand what went wrong, write it on a piece of paper, and tell himself he would not let the same mistake happen again. Then he would slip the paper into the Unhappy Box and close the lid and forget about it!

And so, day by day, Marc grew stronger and stronger and happier and happier. The amazing thing was that after a while, the other children in the class changed, too, because he was such a good example to them and his growing happiness worked like magic! Do you want to know what happened in the end?

Gradually all the children in the class discovered the secret about the Happy Box and asked every day, "Marc, what are you doing today to become happier?"

Marc would share with them what was written on the card. Do you know what happened next? They joined in. In a short time all the children were becoming happier and happier, until in the end all the children in the class were treating each other like friends and being loving and caring for each other.

Oh, it was such a joy to see this happen!

It was just like magic!

Item 12: Responsibility

TC Wants a Dog

By Ruth Liddle

When TC Briggs told his mother he wanted a dog, she looked up from the breakfast table, fixed her big brown eyes on him, and simply shook her head.

"But why not?" he demanded.

"Because I don't want another animal to look after."

"But I would look after it," TC stated emphatically.

"Like you do your goldfish, your hamster and your cat, I suppose," Mrs. Briggs said wearily. "No, I don't think you are ready for the responsibility of owning a dog."

TC looked down at the table. He was feeling guilty. It was true what Mom said. He had enjoyed caring for his other pets when he first got them. But now Mom fed the cat, and he never seemed to remember to feed the fish or the hamster. And nowadays he was always too busy on weekends to clean their homes. TC glanced at the goldfish bowl. The water was so cloudy he could hardly see the fish.

"I'll clean that out tonight," he promised himself. "From now on I'm going to do all my pet chores without being reminded. And I'll do my homework, too. That will show Mom I am more responsible now."

TC didn't mention the subject of the dog again for a few weeks, until one Sunday afternoon. His baby sister was sleeping and his mother was relaxing on the couch.

"It's not that I don't want you to have a dog," Mrs. Briggs explained. "I just don't want to be the one to have to feed it, clean up after it and take it for walks. Owning a dog is a responsibility for the whole of its life—not just a job for a week or two until you get tired of doing it."

"But this would be different, Mom," TC pleaded.

"Maybe," said his mother with a smile. "But I need convincing. You need to show me you are ready for that sort of responsibility. I'll tell you what, you find out what type of dog would make a good family pet, how to train and care for it, and I'll seriously consider getting you one. But you must be very sure you want to take on the responsibility. Remember it's a lifelong commitment."

Leaning over, Mrs. Briggs ruffled TC's hair and gave him a big hug. "I already know you are showing more responsibility at school," she added. "Your teacher called me and said you are the first to hand in your homework these days. Well done. Now, off you go—you've got work to do. Love you!"

"Love you too, Mom!" TC called out as he raced out the door.

"And thanks for cleaning out the fish bowl and remembering to feed the hamster," Mrs. Briggs called after him. But TC was already halfway down the street. His best friend, Mohammed, had just what he needed: a book titled *Caring for Your Pet Dog*.

Mohammed and TC worked together for the rest of the afternoon gathering the facts on dog care, training and different breeds of dogs. TC arranged their findings on note cards and prepared to present them to his mother. Mohammed's mother listened to his presentation. She said it would be okay with her if Mohammed looked after the dog if ever TC and his family were away. "Thanks!" said TC. Now he was sure he had everything he needed.

Mrs. Briggs listened carefully as TC shared his information on dog care and training and told her which dogs would make good pets for a family with a baby and a busy mother.

"Well, TC," his mother responded, "I'm impressed. You certainly know your stuff, and it's a great help to know Mohammed and his mother can help out when we're away."

"There's one more thing, Mom," TC said, passing her a carefully rolled up piece of paper. "Read this."

Mrs. Briggs unrolled the paper and read the promise that had been carefully written in TC's best handwriting:

I, THOMAS CHARLTON BRIGGS, HEREBY PLEDGE TO CARE FOR MY DOG IN A RESPONSIBLE WAY FOR AS LONG AS IT LIVES. Signed, TC Briggs

His mother looked up at him and smiled.

"Well, TC, it looks like we're going to have a dog in the house after all. I can see that you are ready for the responsibility. I'm proud of you."

A few days later, TC became the proud owner of a friendly little dog called Ticka.

Item 13: Responsibility

The Forgotten Garden
By John McConnel

Once upon a time, Ivan, a young man, inherited a garden from his father, a famous master gardener. It was really quite delightful—lavender flowers, blue-green trees, and crystal fountains and streams formed a maze of beauty. A lily pond with winding marble paths led from one visual feast to another. There was always something to appreciate even in the depths of winter, and the scent from carefully chosen plants was delicious. The garden had been created with such love that you could feel the sweetest of vibrations in the air. Everyone who entered the garden was touched with a wave of peace, and the people flocked from miles around to visit the garden because they always left feeling refreshed and happy.

At first, Ivan was thrilled with his inheritance. He loved being in his garden and did his best to look after it. Every morning and evening he spent time clearing the weeds, watering the plants and keeping things in good order. Gradually, however, Ivan began to lose interest in the garden. Many other matters demanded his attention. He took employment in the nearby town and became involved in all sorts of social activities. It was not long before he met a beautiful young woman, Miriam, and eventually they were married and had a family. He neglected the garden, which fell into decay, soon becoming only a distant memory.

In the beginning, the years went by pleasantly enough. Ivan was successful in his business and enjoyed many material trappings—a big house, an expensive car and holidays abroad. However, there was a part of him that was not completely satisfied. Something inside teased his conscience a bit. As the days went by, he began to think frequently about the garden his father had generously bestowed upon him and left in his care. He thought of the sweet scent of the luxurious flowers and the cool taste of the water in his mouth.

One day Ivan decided to visit the garden. The sight that met his eyes made him weep. His precious inheritance had been reduced to a jungle of thorns—the harmony, peace and order of the garden had given way to chaos and confusion. The streams had dried up, the pond was reduced to a puddle, and the shrubs and plants were smothered in creepers. He remembered his father's creation—how it used to be—and he felt ashamed. How could he have let go of something so special? What a fool he had been. At that moment Ivan resolved to restore the garden to its original splendor. Although he had only a vague recollection of how the garden used to be and had very little knowledge of gardening, he set about his task with determination and enthusiasm. In order to increase his knowledge, he took some gardening lessons, researched into the history of the garden, and spoke with anyone who had known his father and the garden.

Armed with the appropriate tools, Ivan began his work. He chopped and burned brambles, removed fallen trees, and retrenched the streams and pond. At first, progress seemed slow, but once the biggest obstacles had been removed, things moved faster. His wife sensed his increasing contentment and joined him in restoring the garden. The original structure of the garden was still there, and most of the shrubs and plants had somehow miraculously survived. They just needed pruning, weeding, nourishing and watering. He and his wife worked long and hard, and their efforts were rewarded.

As each day passed, he felt his love for the garden growing; and the more he loved it, the more it responded to his touch and the easier his efforts became. Word spread that he had come to reclaim his inheritance, and offers of help poured in. Inspired and touched by Ivan's example, many people came to offer their services, and before long, the garden was restored to its former glory. It was a memorial not only to the master gardener, but to the efforts of his son, who, at last, felt complete and satisfied and spent the rest of his days in happiness.

Item 14: Cooperation

A Meteorite Storm Approaches

By John McConnel

"Hold on tight!" shouted Major Yori. "Meteorite storm approaching!" The crew members were at their stations in the blink of an eye. "I reckon we could navigate around the storm if we plot a course something like this," said Major Yori as she continued to instruct the navigation team. She was right. With a couple of tilts and turns, the spaceship changed course and settled into its new direction. Within a few minutes, they had calm sailing again. It was just one of the hazards of space travel.

Far below, on a small planet called Earth, things appeared to be fairly normal—for a little while at least. It happened suddenly. One minute it was a sunny day, and the next minute it was as if someone had turned off the lights, plunging the day into darkness. Some people panicked. Some searched for candles, flashlights and bicycle lights to see with.

At the main space center, the reason for the blackout was visible on a large screen showing pictures sent by Satellite "Fred," which was orbiting Earth. At the tail end of the storm was one huge, enormous, mammoth, gigantic meteorite, almost the size of the planet itself. The meteorite came to a halt just in front of the sun. The people knew that Earth needed the sun to sustain life—plants, animals and humans. This was, therefore, a disaster of terrible proportions, and they needed help.

In the spaceship high above Earth, the transmitter bleeped. Major Yori answered the call and listened to the instructions. Her mission was to destroy the meteorite! At first, her mission seemed impossible. Her ship did not have enough power to shift the huge rock by itself. "What can I do?" she thought. Suddenly, she remembered the long-ago banished spaceship under the command of Captain Zorg. Captain Zorg was the inventor of such deadly weapons that he and his creations had been banished from Earth many years before. Among his inventions was an anti-meteorite missile. Instead of using it to destroy humanity, it could be used to destroy the meteorite threatening humanity! Captain Zorg's super missile was Earth's only hope. But how could he be found and would he help? Yori had serious doubts.

Major Yori urgently but patiently scanned the galaxies, looking for Captain Zorg. Eventually, his ship was found three trillion kilometers away. Contact was made, and after Major Yori had explained the situation to Captain Zorg, he agreed to help save Earth. He had come to understood why the people on

Earth were against his weapons, and he was not bitter over the past. However, by himself, there was not much he could do. He had one anti-meteorite missile on board, but his ship was so old and unsteady that he would not be able to fire it accurately.

Major Yori's ship was steady, but it did not have enough power to launch the rocket by itself. To make matters worse, neither ship had direct access to Satellite "Fred," and so they could not work out the best position from which to safely and successfully launch the missile. Only Ground Control could do that. If Earth were to be saved, everyone would have to work together. There would need to be close cooperation.

The two commanders ordered their ships to come together. They docked safely. The power systems were combined. Contact was made with Ground Control, which guided the two combined ships into position. Captain Zorg carefully prepared the powerful missile for launch and activated the nuclear warhead. The ships zoomed in toward the massive meteorite, and at the precise moment ordered by Ground Control, the deadly weapon was launched.

Zap! Zoom! Pow!

As the two ships hurtled away to safety, there were massive explosions, and the meteorite burst into a million burning bits. On Earth, a huge fireball lit the sky like a wondrous firework. Everyone danced with joy. The mission had been successful. Earth had been saved.

Item 15: Humility

Fairy Story—A Play

By Students at West Kidlington School

Narrator: Once upon a time there were a king and queen. They lived and ruled together happily in a far-off land. They longed to have a child, and one day that dream came true. The Queen gave birth to a lovely son. They named him Rufus. On the day of his birth, the Fairy Godmother visited the King and Queen and said:

Fairy Godmother (FGM): I will grant you any wish for your beautiful new son. Ask and it shall be so.

Queen: We know what we wish for our son.

King: Yes, we wish great wealth for him; he should want for nothing that money can buy.

FGM: Your wish shall be granted.

Narrator: As Prince Rufus grew, he had every toy a boy could wish for. He had anything to drink or eat that he desired. He had every outfit and every sports item imaginable. But no one liked him. He became more selfish and demanding every day.

Rufus: Where is my new tennis racket? I want it now!

Servant One: Shall we play with your train set, Rufus?

Rufus: No! Go find your own train set. You're not sharing mine!

Queen: Oh dear! Where did we go wrong?

Narrator: However, the Queen soon gave birth to a second child, a daughter. They named her Celia. On the day of her birth, the Fairy Godmother visited the King and Queen and said:

FGM: I will grant you any wish for your beautiful new daughter. Ask and it shall be so.

Queen: We know what we wish for our daughter.

King: Yes, we wish that she should have a great talent and so become famous in the land.

FGM: Your wish shall be granted.

Narrator: As Princess Celia grew, she became a wonderful singer and performed in front of the people in the land many times with her beautiful voice. But no one liked her. She had become boastful and big-headed.

Celia: Who cares if I'm late for the concert? They'll wait. I'm much more important than they are, and I have to get my hair just right. Do you think that these shoes really go with this outfit?

Servant Two: Yes, Your Majesty.

Celia: Oh, what would you know? You're just a pathetic servant with no talent at all.

Queen: Oh dear! Where did we go wrong?

Narrator: As time went on the King and Queen put up with their unbearable children, until one day the Queen gave birth to a third child, a daughter. They named her Joy. On the day of her birth, the Fairy Godmother visited the King and Queen and said:

FGM: I will grant you any wish for your beautiful new daughter. Ask and it shall be so.

Queen: We know what we wish for our daughter. We have learned by our mistakes with Rufus and Celia. We wish that she should be the most loving person in the kingdom.

FGM: Your wish shall be granted.

Narrator: As Joy grew, she became such a loving child that her parents loved her dearly in return. She loved animals and nature and all the people she met. Everyone in the kingdom loved her.

Joy: Hello, Mr. Baker. You must be busy. Would you like me to take your dogs for a walk? It's no bother. I'm looking after Katie, and we're going to pick raspberries in the woods.

Mr. Baker: Thank you, that would be a great help. Here are some iced buns to keep you going.

Joy: Oh, thank you. See you later.

Mr. Baker: What a joy she is!

Queen: We should have known. It is not the things a person owns or the talents they possess that make them nice to know and spend time with. It's their good qualities that count.

Item 16: Honesty

The Emperor and the Flower Seeds

Long ago, in this very kingdom, there lived an Emperor who loved nature. Anything he planted burst into bloom. Up came flowers, bushes and even big fruit trees, as if by magic! Of everything in nature, he loved flowers most of all, and he tended his own garden every day. But the Emperor was very old, and he needed to choose a successor to the throne. Who would his successor be? And how would the Emperor decide? As the Emperor loved flowers so much, he decided that flowers would help him choose.

The next day, a proclamation was issued: "All men, women, boys and girls throughout the land are to come to the palace." The news created great excitement throughout the land.

In a village not far from here, there lived a young girl named Serena. Serena had always wanted to visit the palace and see the Emperor, and so she decided to go. She was glad she went. How magnificent the palace was! It was made from gold and was studded with jewels of every color and type—diamonds, rubies, emeralds, opals and amethysts. How the palace gleamed and sparkled! Serena felt that she had always known this place. She walked through the palace doors into the Great Hall, where she was overwhelmed by all the people. It was so noisy. "The whole kingdom must be here!" she thought.

There then came the sound of at least a hundred trumpets, announcing the arrival of the Emperor. All fell silent. The Emperor entered, clutching what looked like a small box. How fine he looked—so noble and elegant! He circled the Great Hall, greeting every person and presenting something to each one. Serena was curious about the small box. "What was inside?" she wondered. "What was he giving to everyone?"

At last, the Emperor reached Serena. She curtsied and then watched as the Emperor reached into the small box and presented her with a flower seed. When Serena received the seed, she became the happiest girl of all.

Then the sound of trumpets filled the Great Hall once more, and all became silent. The Emperor announced: "Whoever can show me the most beautiful flowers in a year's time will succeed me to the throne!"

Serena left for home filled with wonder over the palace and the Emperor, clutching the flower seed carefully in her hand. She was certain she could grow the most beautiful flower. She filled a flowerpot with rich soil, planted the seed carefully and watered it every day. She couldn't wait to see it sprout, grow and blossom into a magnificent flower!

Days passed, but nothing grew in the pot. Serena was worried. She transferred the seed into a bigger pot; filled it with the best quality, richest soil she could find; and watered it twice a day, every day. Days, weeks and months passed, but still nothing happened. By and by the whole year passed. Finally spring came, and it was time to return once more to the palace. Serena was heartbroken that she had no flower to show the Emperor, not even a little sprout. She thought that everyone would laugh at her because all she had to show for the whole year's effort was a pot of lifeless soil! How could she face the Emperor with nothing?

Her friend stopped by on his way to the palace, holding a great big flower. "Serena! You're not going to the Emperor with an empty pot, are you?" said the friend. "Couldn't you grow a great big flower like mine?"

Serena's father, having overheard this, put his arm around Serena and consoled her. "It is up to you whether you go or not," said her father. "You did your best, Serena, and your best is good enough to present to the Emperor."

Even though she felt reluctant to go, Serena also knew she must not disregard the Emperor's wishes. Besides, she also wanted to see the Emperor and the palace again. And so Serena traveled once more to the palace, holding the pot of soil in her hands.

The Emperor was happy to see the Great Hall filled with his subjects, all proudly displaying their beautiful flowers, all eagerly hoping to be chosen. How beautiful all the flowers were! Flowers were of every shape, size and color. The Emperor examined each flower carefully and thoroughly, one by one. Serena, who was hiding in a corner with her head bowed down, wondered how he could choose, since they were all so lovely. Finally, the Emperor came to Serena. She dared not look at the him. "Why did you bring an empty pot?" the Emperor asked Serena.

"Your Majesty," said Serena. "I planted the seed you gave me and I watered it every day, but it didn't sprout. I put it in a better pot with better soil, but still it didn't sprout. I tended it all year long, but nothing grew. So today I brought an empty pot without a flower. It was the best I could do."

When the Emperor heard those words, a smile spread slowly over his face, and he took Serena by the hand. Serena was frightened. She wondered if she were in some sort of trouble.

The Emperor led her to the front of the Great Hall, and turning to the crowd, he exclaimed: "I have found my successor—the person worthy of ruling after me!"

Serena was puzzled. "But, your Majesty," she said, "I have no flower, just this pot of lifeless earth."

"Yes, I expected that," said the Emperor. "From where everyone else got their seeds, I do not know. The seeds I gave everyone last year had all been roasted. It would have been impossible for any of them to grow. Serena, I admire your great courage and honesty to appear before me with the truth. I reward you with my entire kingdom. You will be the next Empress."

NOTE: While effort has been made to report the author of this story, we have learned from Librarian Pam Crowell, Harte Library, Long Beach, California, USA, that there are many versions of this ancient tale, and the original author is unknown.

Item 17: Honesty

The Miner and the Prince
By Lamia El-Dajani

Ali was a miner who used to live with his family in a small house near the jungle. One day, Ali had an accident in the mine. His injuries prevented him from working in the mine. Life then became hard for him and his family. After his injuries began to heal, he started going to the jungle to find a way to feed himself and his family.

One day, Ali was in the jungle sitting beneath a tree, when suddenly he heard the sound of horses running very fast. He saw the Prince riding a horse and behind him a group of soldiers on their horses. They were chasing after a deer. As they disappeared and the forest became quiet again, he saw something on the path that the horses had galloped across. He picked up the object and found it was a very fine leather wallet. The Prince's name was embossed in gold on the front of the wallet. He slowly opened the wallet and saw a large amount of money. Ali remained where he was in the jungle, waiting for the Prince and his soldiers to return so he could give back the wallet. Slowly it became dark. As the night grew late and there was no sign of the Prince, Ali decided to return home.

Ali's wife hurried to meet him, asking him about his day. He excitedly told her what happened and showed her the wallet. She too became very excited and happily said, "This is a gift from God to us."

Ali was surprised. He protested, saying, "This money is not for us. It belongs to the Prince. I found it, so I must return it."

His wife became furious and replied, "The Prince has a lot of money! We are in sore need. We should keep the money for ourselves." She added, more softly, "Especially since we didn't steal the money. We found it in the jungle."

Ali decided not to argue with his wife. He put the wallet in the cupboard and sat with his family and listened as they continued to fuss about the event.

The next day, Ali woke up very early in the morning and slipped from the house before the rest of the family woke up. He took special care not to awaken his wife. He took the bus to the city and searched for the palace. When he reached the palace, the guards stopped him at the gate and prevented him from entering to meet the Prince. He had no appointment. They asked him why he wanted to meet the Prince, but he refused to tell them the reason. He just said that he needed to meet the Prince immediately about an important matter.

"I must meet with the Prince. I will not leave without seeing him," he said.

They pushed him away, but he insisted on seeing the Prince. As the guards began to shout, suddenly the car of the Prince approached the gate. Ali threw himself on the car and called out to the Prince. The Prince opened the window of the car and asked what he wanted. Ali handed the Prince his wallet.

The Prince, looking very surprised, asked Ali where he found it. Ali told him the story of the previous day in the jungle. The Prince then opened his wallet. One could see that he was astonished to find the money untouched. The Prince asked Ali, "Why didn't you take the money?" Ali replied, "I cannot take something that does not belong to me." A gleam of respect appeared in the Prince's eye. The Prince took a large amount of money from the wallet, and with a nod of thanks, gave it to Ali.

Item 18: Honesty

Situation Cards—Honesty

SITUATION CARD–HONESTY

Situation:

Act out the above situation in two ways:

1. Lie about the situation and see what consequences develop.
2. Be honest about the situation and see what happens.

Ask the characters to occasionally freeze their actions so they can tell the audience what their thoughts and fears are.

SITUATION CARD–HONESTY

Situation:

Act out the above situation in two ways:

      1. Lie about the situation and see what consequences develop.

      2. Be honest about the situation and see what happens.

Ask the characters to occasionally freeze their actions so they can tell the audience what their thoughts and fears are.

Item 19: Freedom

The Naughty Little Prince

By Carlos Izquierdo Gonzalez

Eric had red hair, big eyes, and freckles on his face. He was the King's son. But nobody called him Eric; the whole kingdom called him "the naughty little prince." Eric was proud that his father was the King and even prouder that he would be the next King. He always did exactly what he wished without thinking of anyone else. His favorite words were, "As I am the King's son, I am free to do whatever I want, however I want and whenever I want." Eric seemed to use those words in all situations.

When his private teacher asked him if he had finished his homework, Eric answered, "As I am the King's son, I am free to do my homework and study whatever I want, however I want and whenever I want." This attitude from Eric, the naughty little prince, saddened and worried the teacher.

When Eric's friends came to the palace to play, he said, "As I am the King's son, I am free to play whatever I want, however I want and whenever I want." And he would insist on playing only the game he chose. The friends sometimes looked a little sadly at the naughty little prince.

Eric's parents, the King and Queen, were concerned about his behavior and sometimes a bit annoyed. They tried to talk to their son, but each time they did, Eric answered, "As I am your son and will be the future King, I will do whatever I want, however I want and whenever I want." This attitude from Eric saddened and worried his parents. Nobody in the whole kingdom was able to reason with Eric, the naughty little prince.

Eric loved running, jumping and rolling on the grass in the garden of the royal palace. One day, while he was doing whatever he wanted, however he wanted, and whenever he wanted, in the garden of the royal palace, he saw in the distance something shining brightly. Eric was very curious, and so he stopped jumping and rolling, and approached the shiny object. As he came closer, he was surprised to find a tiny imp seated among the thorns of the rosebushes. The imp had a medallion around his neck that shone like a star.

Eric stood above him, and demanded, "Who are you and what are you doing in my palace?"

The imp answered, "I am an imp from the forest. I am rather stuck here among these rosebush thorns. It would be very good of you to help me out."

Eric, the naughty little prince, replied with the words he usually spoke: "As I am the King's son, I am free to get you out of these rosebushes if I want, however I want and whenever I want."

The imp answered, "All right! Look, if you help me out of here, I will give you this shiny medallion around my neck."

"What is that medallion for?" asked Eric.

"This is a magic medallion. It makes people free. If you rub the medallion . . ." the imp started to whisper.

"Rubbish!" impatiently interrupted the naughty little prince. "I am already free. I am the King's son, and I do whatever I want, however I want and whenever I want. But," he continued in a calmer voice, "I do like the shiny medallion, so I will help you out of the rosebush thorns."

So Eric helped the imp of the forest out of the thorns, and the imp placed the medallion in Eric's hand before disappearing.

Eric, happy with his new shining object, came back to the palace and shut himself up in his room. Curious to see what would happen, he held the shining medallion and rubbed it again and again. Within a few moments, however, he began to feel very tired. As his head began to nod and his eyes closed, he fell asleep. The naughty little price began to dream. In the dream, he saw himself grown up. In a wonderful celebration he was crowned as the new King. He was so proud and happy in this dream. But then something began to happen that he did not like at all. Nobody seemed to pay any attention to what he wanted. Each time Eric, the King, gave an order, all his subjects gave the same reply: "We do whatever we want, however we want and whenever we want." All the subjects answered with the same words no matter what he said! Eric was very upset. It was really terrible what was happening. Nobody listened to him. Nobody obeyed him. Everybody did whatever they wanted, however they wanted and whenever they wanted. This attitude from the subjects of his kingdom worried and saddened Eric, the King.

As Eric continued to dream, those same words were repeated by different people all over his land when he asked them to do something. "Oh, no," he thought, "those are my words coming back to me!" Scared, Eric awoke from his dream and ran down the long great hall to find find his parents, the King and Queen.

He ran first to talk to his parents, then to his teacher and then to his friends. He apologized to them all and promised that from that day on, he would change. He explained to each one that he now understood that being free was also being responsible. He and his teacher sat down and had a chat about liberty being like a coin with two sides: on one side you find your rights, and on the other side you find your responsibilities.

In this way, Eric learned a lesson very important in his life. And when he grew up and was crowned, no one even remembered that he had been known as the naughty little prince. Eric, the responsible King, was loved throughout the land.

Item 20: Unity

A Team United

By John McConnel

The manager of the United Soccer Club was in despair. He did not know what to do. A great deal of money had been spent on new team players. After he had hired the players, he dressed them in the most exclusive designer wear and built a very modern stadium. The team, however, was still at the bottom of the league! They had not scored a goal, never mind a match, for months. They were quickly becoming the joke of the soccer world. Television cameramen no longer came to record their matches, and even the fans were staying away.

The problem was that, despite their name, there was no sense of unity in the club. Instead of all working together for the good of the team, each player thought only of himself. The players were always arguing and fighting with each other, both on and off the pitch. The forwards never passed the ball to anyone, but instead tried to score goals by themselves. The defense was all over the place, and the goalkeeper made little effort to save the ball.

The manager grew so frustrated that he decided to seek advice from four wise men who were experienced in soccer. The first wise man told him to chasten the players every time they made a mistake, and then threaten to "sack them" if they did not play any better.

"That's no good," said the manager. "I've been doing that for years and it has not worked."

The second wise man told him to pay the players more money with a big bonus for every goal scored.

"That's no good," said the manager. "They already earn so much money that they don't know what to do with it."

The third wise man said, "What they need is more discipline. Make them train ten hours a day."

"That's no good," said the manager. "If I trained them any more, they would drop dead from exhaustion! They are not machines, you know!"

While the men debated what the manager should do, the fourth wise man kept quiet. His face exhibited traces of thoughtfulness. Finally, he broke his silence and responded to the discussion. He said, "Love is the answer." His voice was gentle, but was filled with conviction and passion. The other men stopped bickering with one another and looked at the fourth man with curiosity.

"I beg your pardon?" said the manager. "Love? What has love got to do with it? I'm not their mother or a saint."

The fourth wise man only smiled with kindness and then began to explain. "Love is the answer to everything. Instead of shouting at the players or criticizing them, try to treat them with respect. Encourage them to focus on one another's strengths, rather than their weaknesses. Tell them to play for the sheer love of the game and to give regard to their fans. Make love your goal and all will be well. Begin by loving and respecting yourself."

The manager went away with a smile on his lips and a twinkle in his eye. He had listened and understood the fourth wise man's words. This whole time he had focused entirely on money. He now began to understand that greed could not bring true satisfaction or lasting happiness.

Over the next few months, the manager worked on loving himself and loving the team. His efforts did not go unrewarded. The arguments stopped and were replaced by laughter and kindness. The players began to share the ball with each other and started to encourage each other when they played. A sense of pride returned to the game. Even the goalkeeper became enthusiastic and determined never to let another ball escape him. The players no longer took their fans for granted. They even began to visit the local schools and youth clubs to show they cared. It was not long before the first goal was scored and a match was won. Once the team was united by love, they were soon on their way.

Item 21: Relaxation/Focusing Exercises

Physical Relaxation Exercise

Sit comfortably . . . and relax. . . . As you relax, let your body feel heavy and focus your attention on your feet. . . . Tighten the muscles for a moment . . . and then relax them. . . . Let them stay relaxed. . . . Now become aware of your legs, letting them be heavy . . . tightening the muscles . . . and then relaxing them. . . . Now the stomach. . . . Tighten the muscles for a moment . . . and then relax them. . . . Free any tension. . . . Be aware of your breathing, and let yourself breathe slowly and deeply. . . . Breathe deeply, letting the air out slowly. . . . Now tighten the muscles in your back and your shoulders . . . and then relax them. . . . Let your hands and arms tighten up . . . and then relax them. . . . Gently move your neck . . . first to one side, then the other. . . . Relax the muscles. . . . Now tighten the muscles of your face . . . your jaw . . . and then relax the face and the jaw. . . . Let the feeling of well-being flow through your body. . . . Focus again on breathing, taking in clear air, letting out any remaining tension. . . . I am relaxed . . . in a state of well-being . . . and ready to be at my best.

—Contributed by Guillermo Simó Kadletz

Peaceful Star Relaxation Exercise

One way to be peaceful is to be silent inside. For a few moments, think of the stars and imagine yourselves to be just like them. They are so beautiful in the sky, and they sparkle and shine. They are so quiet and peaceful. Let your body be still. . . . Relax your toes and legs. . . . Relax your stomach . . . and your shoulders. . . . Relax your arms . . . and your face . . . let the feeling of being safe emerge . . . and a soft light of peace surround you. . . . Inside you are like a beautiful little star. . . . You, the tiny star inside, are full of peaceful light. . . . This light is soft and safe. . . . Relax into that light of peace and love. . . . Let the self be still and peaceful inside. . . . You are focused . . . concentrated. . . . Whenever you want to feel peaceful inside, you can become still . . . content . . . a star of peace.

Garden Image Respect Relaxation Exercise

Sit comfortably and let your body relax. . . . As you breathe slowly, let your mind be still and calm. . . . Starting at your feet, let yourself relax. . . . Relax your legs . . . stomach . . . your shoulders . . . neck . . . your face . . . your nose . . . your eyes . . . and your forehead. . . . Your mind is serene and calm . . . breathe deeply . . . concentrate on stillness. . . . In your mind picture a flower. . . . Imagine the smell. . . . Enjoy its fragrance. . . . Observe its shape and color. . . . Enjoy its beauty. . . . Each person is like a flower. . . . Each one of us is unique . . . yet we have many things in common. . . . Picture a garden around you with many varieties of flowers . . . all of them beautiful. . . . Each flower with its color. . . . Each flower with its fragrance. . . giving the best of itself. . . . Some are tall with pointed petals, some with rounded petals, some are big and others little. . . . Some have many hues of colors. . . . Some attract the eye because of their simplicity. . . . Each one of us is like a beautiful flower. . . . Enjoy the beauty of each one. . . . Each adds beauty to the garden. . . . All are important. . . . Together they form the garden. . . . Each flower has respect for itself. . . . When one respects oneself, it is then easy to respect others. . . . Each one is valuable and unique. . . . With respect, the qualities of others are seen. . . . Perceive what is good in each one. . . . Each has a unique role. . . . Each is important. . . . Let this image fade in your mind, and turn your attention to this room again.

—Contributed by Amadeo Dieste Castejón

Star of Respect Relaxation Exercise

Think of the stars and imagine yourself to be just like them. They are so beautiful in the sky, and they sparkle and shine. . . . They are so quiet and peaceful. . . . Be very still. . . . Relax your toes and legs. . . . Relax your stomach . . . and your shoulders. . . . Relax your arms . . . and your face. . . . Feel safe . . . and allow a soft light of peace to surround you. . . . Inside you are like a beautiful little star . . . you are lovable and capable . . . you are who you are. . . . Each person brings special qualities to the world. . . . You are valuable. . . . Enjoy the feeling of respect inside. . . . You are stars of respect. . . . Let yourself be quiet and peaceful inside. . . . Focus. . . . You are concentrated . . . full of respect . . . content. . . . Slowly bring your attention back to the room.

Sending Love Relaxation Exercise

Be Peace Stars for a few minutes and send love to people all over the world. . . . Think of the stars, and imagine yourself to be just like them. . . . They are so beautiful in the sky, and they sparkle and shine . . . quietly and peacefully. . . . Relax your toes and legs. . . . Relax your stomach . . . and your shoulders. . . . Relax your arms . . . and your face. . . . We are safe. . . . A soft light of peace surrounds you. . . . Inside you are like a beautiful little star. . . . You, the tiny star inside, are full of peaceful light . . . full of love. . . . We can all send love and peace any time we want. . . . Let the self be full of loving energy. . . . Send that love to people all over the world. . . . Let your body relax. . . . Take in more love. . . . You are focused. . . . You are contributing to a better world. . . . Let the mind be still. . . . And then see yourself sitting here again.

Freedom Relaxation Exercise

As we relax, we give our minds the freedom to explore. . . . I imagine that I'm flying through the air . . . like a bird . . . floating on the warm gusts of wind . . . effortlessly . . . feeling free and light. . . . I feel the warm rays of the sun on my back. . . . I am completely free. . . . I let go of any worries and feel light inside . . . no anchors, nothing to stop me . . . and so I fly into the future world . . . and there I find a world of freedom . . . where each person is free . . . content . . . happy. . . . I see students of all races playing together in complete harmony . . . having the freedom of being able to play . . . each respecting the space and time of the other people. . . . In this world, there is respect and love for each person . . . students feel free to make their own choices . . . everything is perfectly balanced. . . . With my mind free from worry, I fly back into the present . . . and I feel free to experience my inner self . . . to appreciate my inner beauty. . . . I am light inside.

—Based on a contribution by Sue Emery

CITED BOOKS AND SONGS

Books

Belloc, Hilaire. *Matilda*. New York: Knopf, 1992. Distributed by Random House.

Cohen, Barbara. *Molly's Pilgrim*. New York: Lothrop, Lee and Shepard Books, 1983.

Gill-Kozul, Carol, Naraine, Gayatri and Strano, Anthony. *Living Values: A Guidebook*. London: Brahma Kumaris, 1995.

Johnson, Spencer. *The Precious Present*. New York: Doubleday, 1984.

Otero, H. "The Two Birds." *Parabolas en son de paz*. Madrid: Editorial CCS, 1993.

Parkinson, Kathy. *The Enormous Turnip*. Niles, Illinois: A. Whitman, 1986.

Ramsay, Barbara. *Finding the Magic*. Syndey: Eternity Ink, 1995. Available through Global Cooperation House, 65 Pound Lane, London NW10 2HH, UK.

Steptoe, John. *Mufaro's Beautiful Daughters, An African Tale*. New York: Lothrop, Lee and Shepard Books, 1987. This was inspired by a folktale collected by G.M. Theal and published in 1895 in his book, *Kaffir Folktales*.

The Boy Who Cried Wolf is sometimes found as a separate illustrated picture book. A facsimile of the 1912 edition is "The Shepherd's Boy and the Wolf." Aesop's Fables. New trans. Jones, V.S. Vernon. New York: Avenel Books. Distributed by Crown Publishers.

309

Universal Declaration of Human Rights—An Adaptation for Children. New York: U.N. Publications, 1992. Sales #E.89.1.19(H) 92-1-100424-1. 46pp. Available at the U.N. Bookstore.

UNESCO. *1995 United Nations Year for Tolerance.* Paris: Office of Public Information, UNESCO, 1995. Available at the U.N. Bookstore.

Visions of a Better World. A United Nations Peace Messenger Publication. London: Brahma Kumaris, 1993.

Songs

Grammer, Red and Kathy. "Teaching Peace." New York: Smilin' Atcha Music, 1986. This cassette has a collection of songs created to help children and their parents break down the "big" idea of World Peace into the individual daily actions that will make it a reality. Available from 939 Orchard Street, Peekskill, New York 10566, USA.

Jackson, Michael. "Heal the World." Epic Record Company.

Lennon, John. "Imagine." Parlophone Record Company. 1971.

Loggins, Kenny. "Conviction of the Heart." *Outside: From the Redwoods.* Columbia, 1993.

Nass, Marcia and Max. Songs for Peacemakers. Educational Activities, Inc., 1993. P.O. Box 392, Freeport, NY 11520 USA. E-mail: *learn@edact.com.* Available from Educational Activities for $11.95 plus shipping.

USA for Africa. "We Are the World." Qwest Record Company.

ACKNOWLEDGMENTS

To the Educators Who Contributed Values Activities

Appreciation to Marcia Maria Lins de Medeiros, who contributed values activities that she created in her work with LVEP in Brazil. Thank you, Marcia Polido, for translating Marcia's activities from Portuguese to English.

Many thanks to Linda Heppenstall and her team at West Kidlington School for their many activities and continuous work. Thank you to all the wonderful educators who contributed activities—Samantha Fraser, Trish Summerfield, Ruth Liddle, Peter Williams, Sue Emery, Natalie Ncube, Ann Stirzaker, Diana Beaver and Tom Bingham. And thank you, Gay Tappen, for your idea of the unifying tree.

Sabine Levy and Pilar Quera Colomina developed activities for children ages six through twelve in *Manual para Educadores II, Valores para Vivir: Una Iniciativa Educativa, Actividades*. The principal author of the manual was Pilar Quera Colomina. Several activities were also drawn from the contributions of Dominique Ache, Encarnación Royo Costa, Teresa Garcia Ramos, Carlos Izquierdo Gonzalez, Guillermo Simó Kadletz and Amadeo Dieste Castejón in this book. The manual was published by the Spanish Committee of UNICEF and the Brahma Kumaris.

Vanda North has been having children do Mind Mapping activities; one event to create thoughts about a peaceful world was held in a football coliseum! Thanks, Vanda. Reference: North, Vanda with Tony Buzan, Get Ahead: Mind Map Your Way to Success. Limited Edition Publishing: Buzan Centre Books, Bournemouth, U.K.

Many appreciative regards to Diana Hsu, John McConnel, Lamia El-Dajani and Wendy Marshall, who heard the request for stories and applied their talents, and Dana Wilkinson for her editorial support with some of the stories.

Thank you, Marcia and Max Nass, for lovingly offering your songs.

Dr. Cicero Prado Sampaio contributed the beautiful images at the beginning of each values unit. Dr. Sampaio is an artist and physician in the south of Brazil.

Thank you, Frow Steeman, for your wonderful cover art work. Ms. Steeman is an artist who lives in Belgium.

Thank you, Carol Gill, for your unlimited enthusiasm and encouragement. Many thanks to Lygia Monteiro, Beverley Crooks, Helen Sayers and Diana Beaver for their suggestions on "de-Americanizing" the text, and to Pam and Jim Crowel for their help in locating stories. Loving appreciation to Diane Holden, Gretchen Krutz, Margaret Keck and Lynn Henshall for their willingness to proofread, and to David Jones for all his help with technology.

Values activities are a cooperative event!

**And thank you to those reading this,
for your interest and dedication to a better world.**

ABOUT THE AUTHOR

Diane G. Tillman is an educational psychologist who worked in a California public school system for twenty-three years. Diane travels all over the world, lecturing on personal development and training educators. She has worked with LVEP since its inception, and she continues to develop content and training materials. She has served with the United Nations Association-USA at the local, regional and national levels.

Living Values Series

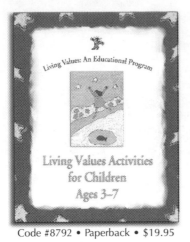

Code #8792 • Paperback • $19.95

Living Values Activities for Children Ages 3–7

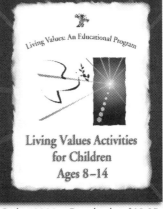

Code #8806 • Paperback • $19.95

Living Values Activities for Children Ages 8–14

Living Values Activities for Young Adults

Code #8814 • Paperback • $19.95

Living Values Parent Groups: A Facilitator Guide

Code #8822 • Paperback • $10.95

Living Values Educator Training Guide

Code #8330 • Paperback • $12.95

To order direct: Phone **800.441.5569** • Online **www.hci-online.com**
Prices do not include shipping and handling. Your response code is **BKS**.

Code #7753 • Paperback • $10.95

"Grieving can be a life-long process that goes through many stages after a trauma has occurred and the headlines are gone. This book picks up where the road forks and provides a path of hope for kids and families who have experienced pain and loss."
—Montel Williams

Every school community experiences losses. Students need to be taught to acknowledge their grief. This book provides a model around this premise and shares stories of other people's losses, as well as the author's interventions with these children and their schools. It also works as a training manual and provides instructions for training a team of people to help students cope with loss.